Elementary
Deductive Logic

ELEMENTARY
DEDUCTIVE LOGIC

HENRY W. JOHNSTONE, JR.

Assistant Professor of Philosophy
The Pennsylvania State University

New York

THOMAS Y. CROWELL COMPANY

1954

MANUFACTURED IN THE UNITED STATES OF AMERICA
BY THE COLONIAL PRESS INC., CLINTON, MASS.

Preface

This brief book stems from the belief that most textbooks of elementary logic are too long. Brevity is achieved primarily by presenting logic as itself exhibiting logical order. The book thus avoids the cumbersomeness involved in treating the various topics of logic as if they were more or less independent of one another. It assumes that students will feel at home in a course in which each topic occupies a definite position in a series proceeding from elementary to advanced material, much as in chemistry, economics, or a foreign language. This sense of security may be contrasted with the impression, frequently characteristic of elementary logic students, that the syllogism and the truth-table are no more than arbitrary selections from an indefinitely large number of loosely related topics, none of which is of much more value than the others. In emphasizing systematic development, this book seeks to preclude that impression.

The present book is brief, also, because it avoids encroaching upon the realm of the instructor. Unlike many current texts, which in effect constitute a set of lectures and deprive the instructor of an essential role, this book attempts to be at most a treatise. Far from eliminating the instructor, it places itself at his disposal.

Deductive logic is the core of almost all courses in elementary logic, and this book covers most of the standard topics of that area. No attempt is made, however, to include inductive logic or the discussion of language. These topics are omitted because there appears to be almost no agreement among teachers of logic either as to exactly what material beyond deductive logic should be covered or as to how it should be studied.   Therefore the option of choosing one's own supplementary material should be welcome.   There are, for example, a number of inexpensive books dealing independently with language and inductive logic, such as L. Susan Stebbing, *Thinking to Some Purpose* (Penguin); James B. Conant, *On Understanding Science* (New American Library); Norman Campbell, *What Is Science?* (Dover); and Monroe C. Beardsley, *Thinking Straight* (Prentice-Hall).   Or the instructor may wish to base this part of the course upon his own lectures.   Or still again, perhaps, as in the case of the author, he will prefer not to supplement at all.

Part Four of this book is especially intended for those who adopt this last alternative, although its use would also be compatible with the decision to supplement.   This part attempts to approach both science and the nature of definition from the point of view of deductive logic.   It may be omitted, however, without detriment to the unity of the book.   So may Sections 16 and 17.   Finally, Section 15, although to some extent presupposed by Part Four, may be omitted by those who regard the diagrammatic treatment of the syllogism as sufficient.

I am indebted to many friends for various kinds of help in preparing this book; especially to Mrs. William K. Du Val, who typed the original draft, and to Professors William Craig, John M. Anderson, John J. O'Connor, and Henry Hiz, who carefully studied parts of the manuscript and gave me indispensable advice.   I trust that the influence of my former logic teachers, Professors Paul Weiss, H. M. Sheffer, C. I. Lewis, and W. V. Quine, is reflected here without too much distortion.

HENRY W. JOHNSTONE, JR.

State College, Pennsylvania
March, 1954

Contents

PART THREE
The Logic of Classes

PART FOUR
Postulates

Elementary
Deductive Logic

1

Introduction

Most textbooks open with a definition of the subject they are intended to cover. The purpose of such a definition is to indicate the nature of material that may be unfamiliar to the reader by referring to ideas that are likely to be more familiar to him. Thus it may be helpful to the student who is unfamiliar with the nature of sociology to be told that it "deals with group behavior, the relationships among men, and the factors entering into and ensuing from these relationships." * In the case of logic, however, it is difficult to begin in this fashion. For although "logic" may be defined, it is not likely that one could define it in terms of ideas already more familiar to the student than that of logic itself. Not that definitions of "logic" are never attempted. A common one is that it is "the study of necessary inference." This statement may well be true, but it would hardly be illuminating to a person just beginning to study logic. Most people can distinguish a logical argument from an illogical one without having the slightest idea what is meant by a "necessary inference," and if they are incapable of making that distinction, it is doubtful whether this phrase or any other would be of much assistance to them.

In a sense, however, this entire book is an attempt to define

* Samuel Smith, "Introduction," in *New Outline of the Principles of Sociology* (Ed. by Alfred McClung Lee), New York, Barnes & Noble, Inc., 1951, p. v.

"logic." While it presupposes that the student already possesses an idea of what logic is about, it aims to clarify this idea. One of the purposes of studying logic is to be able to make a sharp distinction between the problems capable of being solved by logic and those falling within other disciplines. For the correct identification of a problem is the first step toward its solution. But in order to decide whether a given problem is logical or not, one must be sure what logic includes, and what it excludes. This book, in particular in Parts One and Four, is intended to illuminate both the scope and the limitations of logic. It is a definition of "logic" in the sense of making the subject matter of logic more definite.

Once a problem has been correctly identified as soluble by logic, we need to know precisely what methods to apply to it. In Parts Two and Three, all the important elementary techniques of deductive* logic are enumerated. But it must be emphasized that no technique is *merely* enumerated. That procedure would suggest that the order of the topics was a matter of no special consequence, when, in fact, the reverse is true; to understand any topic (except the first) discussed in the book requires previous understanding of those that precede it. The organization is a systematic, proceeding from elementary material to advanced. This does not mean that the book consists of a series of increasingly complicated theorems, as in plane geometry. But it does mean that the reader will have difficulty comprehending the content of Part Two without familiarity with Part One, or that of Section 16 apart from that of Section 15. In this respect, the present work compares with a textbook in science.

The four parts into which this book is divided represent the major phases of the systematic progression from elementary to advanced material. Part One, "The Nature of Logic," defines the fundamental ideas involved in the solution of all logical problems, ideas such as those of *proposition, logical truth, argument, valid argument,* and *implication.* These definitions yield the vocabulary

---

* The distinction between "deductive" logic and logic that is not deductive cannot be made clear until somewhat later (page 20).

common to all the later parts and are necessary for an understanding of these parts. No specific methods for solving logical problems as such are presented in Part One, but the basic principles governing all the techniques to be developed later are stated here. And the definitions of fundamental ideas make it possible later on to describe these techniques with precision.

Part Two, "The Logic of Propositions," deals with methods for solving logical problems of a relatively simple sort. Various techniques are described for testing the validity of arguments of a certain general type. At the end of the part, all of these techniques are shown to give way to use of what are called "truth-tables."

Part Three, "The Logic of Classes," is concerned with problems of a somewhat more complicated nature. It widens the area of those arguments whose validity is open to examination. But it makes no claim to provide a basis for examining *all* arguments; this lies beyond the scope of the present book, if not beyond that of human knowledge altogether. The most important technique described in Part Three is that of applying the rules of the Syllogism; but certain other techniques introduced in this part are not necessarily reducible to the application of these rules.

Part Four, "Postulates," does not follow up Part Three as that part did its predecessor. Part Four does not attempt to solve any problems beyond the depth of those discussed in previous parts; instead, it treats of a general application of logic to organized knowledge in both science and everyday life. The theory of the Syllogism as presented in Part Three is used as an example of such organized knowledge. The part ends with a discussion of the more significant considerations involved in framing a definition. Most of the general principles and some of the specific techniques explained in the three preceding parts are presupposed by Part Four.

PART ONE

The Nature of Logic

2

Propositions

The units of logic are *propositions*.   A proposition is whatever a declarative sentence declares to be true or false.   The sentence "Chicago is west of New York," for example, expresses the proposition *that* Chicago is west of New York; this is what the sentence asserts to be true.   The same proposition may be expressed by the synonymous declarative sentence "New York is east of Chicago." In general, a proposition is a meaning capable of being expressed by more than one declarative sentence, for there are almost always alternative ways of phrasing a given truth or falsehood.   "The cat is black" and "Le chat est noir" have almost nothing in common except the proposition they both express.

Only declarative sentences express propositions; exclamatory, hortatory, optative, and imperative sentences do not.   Nothing is asserted to be true or false by such sentences as "Block that kick," "Let x be the speed of the current," or "Column left, march!" Nor do isolated nouns or adjectives usually express propositions; "Desk," for instance, fails to specify what is supposed to be true or false of a desk.   The exclamation "Gold!" might be an exception to this rule; the speaker may be asserting what would be false if uttered in the presence of iron pyrite.   But almost any generalization about propositions has an exception; there is no universal rule for determining whether a given word or sentence expresses a proposition, or, for that matter, whether two sentences express the same proposition. But similarly, there is no absolute criterion for determining whether a given sentence expresses a lie, or an insult. The student who understands that this discussion of propositions is itself an expression of propositions rather than mere wishes or commands will understand the meaning of "proposition" as well as he needs to for any purpose of this course.

For technical purposes, a distinction is often made between *simple,* or *atomic,* propositions, and those that are *complex,* or *molecular.* A proposition is complex when one or more of its components is itself a proposition; otherwise, it is simple. Thus "If it rained, the game was to be called" is complex, having as it does the two propositional components, "It rained" and "The game was to be called." But each of these components is itself simple; no part of "It rained," for example, is a proposition. "The coach believed that the game was to be called" also expresses a complex proposition; for it contains as a part "The game was to be called." We shall make use of this distinction in the sequel.

The notion of a proposition raises certain general questions. One of these concerns the residue of meaning which each sentence seems to carry individually, and which cannot be construed as a proposition. Consider the two sentences "Jones is dead" and "Jones is no longer living." Insofar as these two sentences are true or false, they both express precisely the same proposition. But insofar as these sentences enter into discourse among civilized men, they differ in use. The first is blunt; one would not ordinarily use this mode of expression in referring to a man who had recently passed away and with whom one had felt some bond. In such a case, the second would be preferable. Thus the two sentences differ by what might be called "a shade of meaning." In general, any two distinct sentences expressing the same proposition will differ by such a shade—a shade which it is important to select correctly in polite intercourse and advertising, as well as in poetry and other forms of literature. If these differential hues of meaning are an identifiable factor of sentences expressing propositions, they are of dominant significance for imperative and optative sentences, which do not express propositions.

The discipline which attempts to investigate and classify nonpropositional meanings used to be known as "rhetoric," but in modern parlance falls within the field called "semantics." There are several "schools" of Semantics, and many lively issues among them. Semantics, however, will not be discussed in this book. We shall instead confine our attention to that study of the propositional meanings of declarative sentences which has, through the ages, been called "logic."

EXERCISES

A. Which of the following sentences express propositions? Which express complex propositions?

1. Do not walk on the grass.
2. If you walk on the grass you will be fined.
3. To walk on the grass is to violate the law.
4. Let's walk on the grass.
5. I want to walk on the grass.
6. Philadelphia is a large city.
7. What a large city Philadelphia is!
8. Philadelphia is large, but New York is larger.
9. How large is Philadelphia?
10. I must find out the size of Philadelphia.
11. The year is 1984.
12. Imagine that the year is 1984.
13. Can't you imagine that the year is 1984?
14. You seem incapable of imagining that the year is 1984.
15. Let the year be 1964, then.
16. Please do not ask me any questions.
17. If you ask me no questions I will tell you no lies.
18. You may ask me all the questions you want to, but I cannot guarantee the truth of the answers.
19. How many more of your impertinent questions must I tolerate?
20. How many more of your impertinent questions I am going to tolerate, you'll soon find out.

B. Which of the following sentences express essentially the same proposition as the one expressed by *"Boggs will be late to class today"?*

1. Boggs must have overslept today.
2. Boggs will be put on probation tomorrow.
3. Boggs will not get to class on time today.
4. Boggs never gets to class on time.
5. If Boggs gets to class on time today, then anything is possible.
6. Boggs was just coming out of the dormitory at 9:05 today.
7. The prof will be furious if Boggs comes in late again.
8. Whoever says that Boggs will be late to class today is telling the truth.
9. Boggs will not get to class early today.
10. Boggs can avoid being late to class today only by using his roommate's motorcycle.

SUPPLEMENTARY READINGS

1. Alice Ambrose and Morris Lazerowitz, *Fundamentals of Symbolic Logic,* New York, Rinehart & Company, Inc., 1948, Sec. 6.

2. Morris R. Cohen and Ernest Nagel, *An Introduction to Logic and Scientific Method,* New York, Harcourt, Brace and Company, 1934, Ch. II, Sec. 1.

3. Ralph M. Eaton, *General Logic,* New York, Charles Scribner's Sons, 1931, Pt. I, Sec. 3.

3

Factual and Logical Propositions

It is possible now to take a small but important step toward the identification of the nature of logic. This step depends upon the recognition of two different kinds of propositions. Propositions of the first kind are true or false by virtue of some fact, situation, circumstance, or state of affairs. Propositions of the second kind are true or false independently of anything actually existing; their truth or falsity depends upon no fact, situation, circumstance, or state of affairs whatever. Propositions of the first kind are called *factual;* those of the second kind are called *logical*.

These two kinds of propositions are easy to exemplify. Factual propositions constitute nearly all of our discourse. They predominate in science and literature as well as in everyday speech. All of the following propositions are factual:

(3.1) Bats are mammals.
(3.2) It is raining.
(3.3) Today is Monday.
(3.4) All men are mortal.
(3.5) Some black cats are male.

Special attention is called to the fact that not all of these propositions are necessarily true. Perhaps it is not now raining; today may not be Monday. But a factual proposition need not be true, either now or at any time. All that is required of such a proposition is that its truth or falsity must depend upon some fact or situation.   This is the case for each of the propositions above. The truth of 3.1, for instance, depends on the fact that bats are indeed mammals; this is a circumstance that zoologists have verified.   If 3.2 is true, it will be so by virtue of a certain meteorological state of affairs—falling raindrops; if it is false, its falsity depends upon the absence of raindrops.   Proposition 3.4 is true by virtue of a biological fact, or false in view of a theological fact.

Note that although the relevant facts are unavailable, a given proposition may yet be factual.   "There is oil under The White House" is an example of this sort of proposition; one knows what fact *would* substantiate it.   Even where there is disagreement as to what *sort* of fact would confirm a given proposition, that proposition is factual as long as there is agreement that *some* fact would confirm or confute it.   A case in point would be "Mars is inhabited."   Predictions, hypotheses, and speculations are generally factual propositions.   Finally, whatever assertions are made in the interest of make-believe are factual by virtue of agreeing or disagreeing with a fictitious body of "facts" in whose existence one is willing to believe for the moment.

Factual propositions so preponderate in ordinary discourse that we may be unaware of logical propositions, which are true or false without regard to facts.   Examples of the latter are

(3.6)   Bats are either mammals or not mammals.
(3.7)   It is not both raining and not raining.
(3.8)   If today is Monday, tomorrow is Tuesday.
(3.9)   If Socrates is a man and all men are mortal, then Socrates is mortal.
(3.10)   All black cats are black.

The student may be puzzled by the attention paid to such trivial propositions.   But for the present let us consider in precisely what sense they are "trivial."   Their triviality consists in the fact that they convey no information about our actual world.   For example, proposition 3.6 ascribes no zoological property to bats.   For that matter, it does not even convey the information that bats exist; it would be true of a world from which bats were absent. And 3.7 tells the reader nothing about the weather which is now occurring. To find out whether it is raining, we might properly call up the Weather Bureau; consider, however, the propriety of inquiring whether, at the present moment, it is true that it is not both raining and not raining! Again, 3.9 describes no feature of our world; its truth does not depend on the actual existence of Socrates, men in general, or mortal beings.

A true logical proposition, then, is true independently of any fact, situation, circumstance, or state of affairs. When it is false, its falsity likewise exhibits no dependence upon an actual world. Thus, "Bats are both mammals and not mammals," "Today is Monday and tomorrow is Wednesday," and "Some black cats are not black," are false for all times and places, and our knowledge of their falsity does not depend upon any factual information we may have. Whereas the scope of a factual proposition is confined to this world, a true logical proposition is true for all possible worlds; and a false logical proposition is false for all possible worlds, or true for no world that could possibly exist.

How do we recognize a logical proposition as such? Obviously, we need not review all possible worlds in order to satisfy ourselves that "All black cats are black" is true of all possible worlds; we need not have every fact at our command to perceive that the proposition is independent of every fact. The mark by which we invariably recognize a logical proposition when we meet one is its peculiar form or structure. In its form resides its very triviality. In the next section we shall have to consider what aspects of its form render a proposition logical.

Theoretically, every proposition is either factual or logical, and none is both. In practice, however, there will inevitably be borderline cases where the proper classification is doubtful. "All squares are squares" is quite clearly logical, but the status of "All squares are rectangles" depends upon what we mean by "square." If our definition of "square" already involves the concept of a rectangle, the proposition is logical; otherwise, it is not. Particular meanings of words are, in fact, indispensable to our interpretation of propositions as logical; *a word must have the same meaning wherever it occurs in a logical proposition.* Indeed, unless we make this assumption, there can be no logical propositions at all, either true or false, and thus, no such thing as the study of logic. For example, by a play on the meaning of the word "rain" it might be both raining and not raining—raining in New York but not in Philadelphia. But what, precisely, is meant by "the same meaning" is far from clear. Just as there is no hard-and-fast rule for identifying propositions, so there is no formula for deciding in all cases whether a given proposition is factual or logical. We are dealing here with ideas so general and so abstract that any detailed specification of them would be arbitrary. The question "Under what conditions is a proposition logical rather than factual?" is like the question "Under what conditions is a series of sentences poetry rather than prose?" For while there is ideally a clear-cut distinction between poetry and prose, many specimens of writing are notably difficult to classify and any objective procedure for doing so will produce at least some results which seem arbitrary.

EXERCISE

Which of the following propositions are logical?

1. All men are created equal.
2. If Boggs is equal to Diggs, then Diggs is equal to Boggs.
3. A rose is a rose.
4. A rose is a flower.
5. All bodies are affected by gravity.
6. All bodies are both affected by gravity and not affected by gravity.
7. Every event has a cause.
8. The same particular cause always produces the same particular effect.
9. Either Boggs is my friend or Boggs is not my friend.
10. Either Boggs is my friend or Boggs is my enemy.
11. If some Senators are women, then this is an enlightened country.

12. If some Senators are women, then some women are Senators.
13. No book is both rectangular and not rectangular.
14. All books are either rectangular or not rectangular.
15. If it is either raining or snowing, it will be difficult to drive.
16. If it is either raining or snowing, and it is not raining, then it is snowing.
17. It is either raining or not raining.
18. It is either raining or snowing.
19. All heavy bodies fall when not supported.
20. If all heavy bodies fall when not supported, and a flatiron is a heavy body, then a flatiron falls when not supported.
21. Virtue is its own reward.
22. If all virtuous acts are rewarded, and saving a life is a virtuous act, then saving a life will be rewarded.
23. No one lives forever.
24. No one lives forever, but some live forever.
25. If no one lives forever, then some do not live forever.

SUPPLEMENTARY READING

W. V. Quine, *Mathematical Logic,* New York, W. W. Norton Company, Inc., 1940, "Introduction."

4

The Anatomy of Logical Propositions

We return now to the issues which are of greatest consequence for the present inquiry. In Section 3 it was indicated that the truth or falsity of a proposition which is logically true or logically false depends entirely upon the form or structure of the proposition. What, precisely, does this mean?

An important characteristic of any logically true proposition is that some of the words used to express it may be replaced by any word whatsoever belonging to the same part of speech, and yet the proposition remains logically true. Consider 3.6 (page 12). If we replace "mammals" by "reptiles," we obtain "Bats are either reptiles or not reptiles," which is a logically true proposition. Similarly, the truth of 3.6 will not be affected if we substitute "insects," "fossils," "mythical creatures," or even "saucepans" for "mammals." We might schematize this result as follows:

(4.1) Bats are either ——— or not ———.

Proposition 4.1 is now true no matter what plural noun is used to fill the blank. (A plural noun—or perhaps an adjective—is, of course, called for to preserve the grammatical form of the sentence expressing 4.1. If a word belonging to some other part of speech —say, an adverb—were supplied, 4.1 would become meaningless, and thus neither true nor false. Consider, for instance, "Bats are either *too* or not *too*.")

16

But this does not complete the project. For the truth of 4.1 depends in no way upon its containing the word "bats." Suppose, in this proposition, we substitute "mice" for "bats." We obtain

(4.2) Mice are either ———— or not ————,

which, again, is logically true regardless of how the blanks are filled. We can write "books," "tables," "ice cream cones," or even "Rotarians," instead of "bats"; the result is still logically true. Thus, "bats" may be replaced by a blank of a new sort, which may be filled by any plural noun. The outcome is

(4.3) ***** are either ———— or not ————.

Proposition 4.3 is a form of the Law of the Excluded Middle, an important truth of logic to be discussed in detail in later sections.

Let us assure ourselves that no further word in 4.3 is replaceable by a blank. "Either" and "or" are correlative; they function as a single word. If the word "and," or its correlative form "both . . . and," is substituted, 4.3 is transformed into a falsehood. For the proposition

(4.4) ***** are both ———— and not ————

is no longer logically true; it is, in fact, false for all substitutions for the blanks, and is therefore logically false. So "either . . . or" is at least one constituent of 4.3 the replacement of which will remove that proposition from the realm of propositions true independently of any fact or state of affairs.

Similarly, the substitution of "indeed" for "not" in 4.3 reveals that "not" is indispensable to the logical truth of 4.3. For consider the resulting proposition

(4.5) ***** are either ———— or indeed ————.

Common sense dictates that "either ———— or indeed ————" contracts simply to "————" (for example, "either red or indeed red" means, precisely, "red"); this contraction will be justified in Part Two. In any event, 4.5 reduces to

(4.6) ***** are ————.

The truth of the proposition as expressed by 4.6 is no longer independent of any fact or situation. When the blanks are filled in, it will be a factual proposition; for example, "Bats are mammals," or "Ants are rational." The truth or falsity of such a proposition will depend upon some feature of the actual world. A factual proposition results, in the same fashion, from the substitution of some other word for "are."

Three words of proposition 4.3, then, are necessary to its status as a logically true proposition: "either . . . or," "not," and "are." Their necessity consists in the fact that not every other word may be substituted for any of these without changing 4.3 from a logical truth into a logical falsehood or a factual proposition. Proposition 4.3 is, then, logically true only because it contains these words in the precise positions they occupy. And these words are unlike the others, for which any word belonging to the same part of speech might be substituted without changing the proposition from a logical truth into anything else. Let us call words like "either . . . or," "are," and "not," *essential words,* or *constants,* to represent the fact that there is a logical truth to which they are essential. And let us call any word which may be used to fill either sort of blank in 4.3 an *inessential word,* or *variable.*

Propositions 3.7 to 3.10 of the list given in Section 3 may be analyzed by the method used for 3.6. We do not at present have the equipment actually to analyze all of them; we can, however, deal satisfactorily with 3.7, 3.9, and 3.10 (page 12). These reduce, respectively, to the following logical truths:

(4.7) Not both ———— and not ————.
(4.8) If ———— is a ***** and all ***** are /////, then ———— is
        /////.
(4.9) All ———— ***** are ————.

Notice that in 4.7 the blank must be replaced by a proposition as a whole. "Not both bats and not bats" is not a complete sentence; at a minimum, a form like "Not both it is raining and it is not raining" (colloquially, "It is not both raining and not raining") is required for completeness. This sets 4.7 apart from all the other examples we have been considering; for in these, the blanks all stand for nouns or adjectives. Logical truths like 4.7 are to be the special subject of Part Two.

In everyday language, logical truths are often called "self-evident statements," and a logical falsehood is characterized as "self-contradictory." But these terms are somewhat more inclusive than the phrases we have adopted, since, for example, propositions which are not, strictly speaking, logically true are sometimes called "self-evident," as in the opening passage of The Declaration of Independence.

The material of this section affords us an opportunity to make several general statements about logic, although any such statement must, at this stage of the exposition, be rough and approximate. The most obvious of these is based on the procedure we have employed in analyzing our examples. *Logic,* we may say, *is the analysis of logical propositions.* (This statement may seem to be circular or redundant, but it actually conforms to the standards of good definition, since "logical proposition" has already been defined quite independently of this definition of "logic." A later investigation of the general process of defining terms should throw light on this matter.) By "analysis" here, we mean more than the mere exhibition of the forms of particular propositions; logic attempts not only to reveal the specific configuration of essential words by virtue of which a given proposition is a logical truth, but also to make generalizations about such configurations. What techniques, in general, are available for showing that a given proposition is or is not logically true? The effort to answer this question, as well as to exhibit particular structures, is an important aspect of the analysis of logical propositions, and one which will occupy us throughout the next two parts.

Another statement about the nature of logic is based on the words which are commonly essential to logically true propositions. Among these words are "either . . . or," "not," "and," "if . . . then," "are" (or "is"), "all," and "some." Logic might therefore be characterized as *the study of the behavior of the words essential to logically true propositions.* Such a study is more than a mere catalogue of essential words. It is, for the most part, an endeavor to define these words in terms of each other, and to show, in general, how they occur in logical truths. The succeeding parts may be construed as an endeavor of this sort.

It becomes important at this point to refer to the title of this book. The statements we have just made are supposed only to express the nature of the enterprise which has commonly been called *deductive logic.* Deductive logic is wholly distinct from the study which has received the somewhat misleading name of "inductive logic." While the former analyzes propositions which are logically true or false, the latter is not essentially concerned with propositions of this sort, but focuses its attention instead upon those which are factual. To put the matter briefly, inductive logic is the attempt to justify such scientific generalizations as "All salt is soluble," "The period of a pendulum depends only on its length," and "Smoking decreases longevity." Such generalizations are completely unlike the logical propositions which deductive logic considers, in that they are informative rather than trivial; probable at best, instead of certain; and dependent for their truth or falsity on some feature of the actual world without being true or false in all possible worlds. To make this distinction explicit, however, is not to disparage the role of inductive logic. Science is impossible unless it accepts certain definite criteria for the truth or falsity of its generalizations. But the reader is advised to regard the word "logic" as it appears in the phrase "inductive logic" as entirely distinct from, and at best a homonym of, the "logic" in "deductive logic."

EXERCISE

Each of the propositions below is logically true.

A. Which are its essential words or constants?

B. Which are its inessential words or variables? Show how another word may be substituted for each variable without changing the proposition from true to false, false to true, or logical to factual. Indicate in each case whether the variables are *propositions as a whole* or *nouns or adjectives*.

Sample: All black cats are black. A. Constants: "all," "are." B. Variables: "black," "cats." Substitute "bald" for "black" and "men" for "cats." "All bald men are bald." Variables must be *nouns or adjectives*.

1. Either Boggs goes fishing or Boggs does not go fishing.
2. All triangles are either isosceles or not isosceles.
3. If it is not the case both that it is noon and that my watch is right, and it is noon, then my watch is not right. (*Hint:* Treat "it is not the case . . . that" as a single constant.)
4. If nothing is both solid and liquid, and cobalt is solid, then cobalt is not liquid.
5. Either some chimpanzees are intelligent or no chimpanzees are intelligent.
6. If either some chimpanzees are intelligent or some psychologists are mistaken, and it is not the case that some chimpanzees are intelligent, then some psychologists are mistaken.
7. If it is not the case that some chimpanzees are intelligent, then no chimpanzees are intelligent.
8. Nothing is both solid and not solid.
9. Everything is either solid or not solid.
10. If all swans are white, and some birds are not white, then some birds are not swans.
11. Either Diggs is fated to pass the course or Diggs is not fated to pass the course.
12. If no fish is a mammal, then no mammal is a fish.
13. If not all mammals are carnivorous then some mammals are not carnivorous.
14. If the mail comes only when it is not a holiday, and it is a holiday, then the mail does not come.
15. If 5 is greater than 2, then 2 is not greater than 5.
16. Whoever washes the dishes does not go to the movies; therefore, whoever goes to the movies does not wash the dishes.
17. All carnivores are mammals, and all cats are carnivores; therefore, all cats are mammals.
18. Either all tomatoes are red or some tomatoes are not red.
19. All birds fly, but no fish flies; therefore, no fish is a bird.
20. If everything is blue, then something is blue.

SUPPLEMENTARY READINGS

1. Alfred Tarski, *Introduction to Logic and the Methodology of Deductive Sciences,* New York, Oxford University Press, 1941, Sec. 1-2.

2. W. V. Quine, *Mathematical Logic,* New York, W. W. Norton Company, Inc., 1940, "Introduction."

3. Alice Ambrose and Morris Lazerowitz, *Fundamentals of Symbolic Logic,* New York, Rinehart & Company, Inc., 1948, Sec. 8.

5

Implication and Inference

In Section 2 (page 8), we distinguished between "simple" and "complex" propositions. This distinction enables us to define the fundamental notion of an *argument*. By "an argument" we shall mean "a complex proposition one of whose constituent propositions is represented as a conclusion following from the others." At the very least, then, an argument will involve a proposition argued *from* and a proposition argued *to:* a *premise* and a *conclusion.* Thus in the argument "Since today is a holiday, there are no classes," the premise is "today is a holiday," and the conclusion is "there are no classes." Most arguments involve more than one premise; in fact, the one just cited must implicitly assume "there are no classes on holidays" as a supplementary premise if it is to be beyond criticism. Further examples of arguments are

(5.1) Since Boggs is not in class, he must be sick.
(5.2) Since Boggs is not in class, he must be in Antarctica.
(5.3) Since Boggs is a senior, and all seniors must pose for yearbook portraits, Boggs must pose for a yearbook portrait.

The contrast between 5.1 and 5.2 is intended to show that an argument does not lose its status as an argument merely because it is unreasonable. Arguments as such may be either strong or weak. All that is essentially required of an argument is that its conclusion is *represented* as following from its premises. The

23

arguer makes this representation; the argument is no more than his
claim that the premises constitute sufficient evidence to warrant the
conclusion.   Whether this claim is, in any particular case, justified,
is another matter—and a fundamental concern of logic.

Arguments may be either factual or logical propositions, as a
comparison between 5.3 on the one hand and 5.1 and 5.2 on the
other will reveal.   For 5.3 contains the variables "Boggs," "senior," and "must pose for a yearbook portrait," while 5.1 and 5.2
contain no variables, but derive their truth or falsity from facts.

Notice that the ordinary usage of the word "argument" involves
at least one important meaning which the definition we have given
above does not suggest and is not intended to suggest, the meaning
"debate" or "controversy."   While arguments, in the logical sense,
may be used in controversies, they need not be.   For our purposes, a person might argue all by himself, provided only that he
were attempting to establish a conclusion.

We have defined an argument in terms of its use, rather than by
referring to its form.   It is a mistake to suppose that the conclusion or premises of an argument can be identified merely through
formal considerations such as, for example, their grammatical order in the argument.   While there are many arguments (including
5.1, 5.2, and 5.3) in which the conclusion occurs last, this is by no
means necessarily the case.   The following inversions of 5.1 and
5.3 indicate that the conclusion might well occur at the beginning
or in the middle:

(5.4) Boggs must be sick, since he is not in class.
(5.5) Since Boggs is a senior, he must pose for a yearbook portrait;
       for all seniors must pose for yearbook portraits.

A more reliable (but, again, not infallible) way of identifying
the premises and conclusion of an argument arises from an understanding of the force of certain words which often occur in arguments.   Words like "since," "for," and "because" almost invariably precede a premise of an argument, as in 5.5.   "Therefore,"
"thus," "hence," and "so," on the other hand, are usually followed

by the conclusion. But the occurrence of any of these words is not essential to an argument; what *is* essential is the arguer's claim to have established a conclusion. To identify the conclusion with certainty, we should have to be acquainted with the intentions of the arguer in question, and this is not always possible.

Two basic concepts of logic, the concepts of *implication* and of *inference,* can be made clear if we reflect further on the intentions of a person who uses an argument. One of his intentions is to exhibit the premises as supporting the conclusion. What, precisely, does the arguer claim? One reply is that he claims that *the premises are sufficient to establish the conclusion,* or that *if the premises are true, the conclusion must be true.* From the point of view of logic, this claim may be restated by saying that the arguer claims that *the premises imply the conclusion,* or that *there is a relation of implication between the premises and the conclusion.*

It has already been pointed out that this claim may or may not be justified. If the premises do imply the conclusion, it is justified; otherwise, it is not. Implication is a relation among propositions in themselves—a relation which either exists or fails to exist between any given pair of propositions regardless of what anyone may think or claim. One proposition may well imply another even when no one is aware of it. While only humans argue, only propositions imply. Later (in Section 7) we shall return to the concept of implication and try to describe it with greater precision.

While the arguer does attempt to establish that the premises of his argument imply its conclusion, this attempt is not his only concern in arguing. Another important intention on the part of anyone who uses an argument is *to establish the conclusion as a matter of information.* Implication as such does not provide that information. "*X* implies *Y*" does not tell us that *Y* in itself is true; it only tells us that *Y* must be true *if X* is true. And this hypothetical sort of knowledge is generally insufficient for purposes of concrete action. For example, the person who argues, as in 5.1, that *since* Boggs is not in class, he must be sick presumably means more than merely that *if* Boggs is not in class, he must be sick.   On the basis of the former statement a concrete act, such as telephoning the infirmary, would be warranted; on the basis of the latter it would not be, for *"if* Boggs is not in class, he must be sick" might be true even when Boggs *is* in class and is *not* sick.   The difference here may be expressed by saying that the person who argues as in 5.1 not only supposes that the premises *imply* the conclusion, but also intends to *infer* the conclusion.

As we have said, implication is a bridge between two proposi- tions.   In *inference*—the process of inferring—the arguer crosses the bridge from premises to conclusion.   In order to do this, he must begin by occupying a position on the "premises" side of the bridge; he must, to speak in straightforward language, affirm the truth of the premises.   Thus whoever wishes to cross the bridge of implication involved in "If Boggs is not in class, he must be sick" to the conclusion that Boggs is sick must be willing to de- clare that Boggs is not in class. *Inference, then, is that feature of any argument which may be characterized by saying that the arguer has, in effect, affirmed the premises, and thereby the con- clusion.*   Inference is often called "demonstration," "deduction," or "proof."

From this discussion of implication and inference a point of central importance emerges: *not every proposition can be proved.* Proof, or inference, assumes a situation in which premises imply conclusion; the conclusion is then proved when the premises are asserted.   Now if these premises are simply asserted, but not themselves proved, then at least one proposition remains unproved. We might try to prove the premises themselves.   In order to do so, we shall have to elicit some further set of propositions which imply the premises in question, and which can themselves be asserted.   But this new set of propositions will itself have to be proved if *everything* is to be proved; and the process goes on without end.   One is finally forced to admit some fundamental premise which remains unproved.

Let us reiterate this point in symbols.   Let s be a proposition which we wish to prove.   In order to accomplish this proof, we must find a premise (or set of premises) *r*, which implies *s*, and which we can assert. But if we are out to prove *every* proposition, we must prove *r*, too; we cannot merely assert *r* without proof. Let us assume that we can find some argument having at least one new proposition *q* as its premise, and r as its conclusion. Then by asserting *q* we have proved *r*. But, to prove *q* itself, we shall have to discover at least one premise *p* which implies it and which we can assert—and so on to infinity. At some juncture in any discipline we must be prepared to settle for a basic premise the assertion of which is a matter of faith. Such basic premises will be scrutinized in Part Four, which deals with the theory of postulates. Meanwhile, it is important to see that the principle that *not everything can be proved* has, as its corollary, the law that *nothing can be proved unless something is assumed without proof.* For it is only through the unproved assumption of *r*, or *q*, or some proposition further along the line, that the chain of implications can be broken in such a way as to permit the unqualified assertion of *s*.

This section has made no use of the distinction between logical and factual propositions. The premises or conclusion of an argument may be either logical or factual, as may the argument as a whole. In Section 6, the theme of logical truth will re-enter the discussion, and will thenceforth dominate this book; in particular, we shall be focusing our attention on arguments which are logically true.

For the moment, however, it is necessary to emphasize that the dictum, "not every proposition can be proved," holds good in spite of the existence of logically true propositions. It may be thought that the proof of all propositions could be carried out, if only one could discover appropriate logical truths to serve as the basic premises. One might hope, perhaps that the "self-evidence" of such premises would warrant the assertion of whatever conclusions might be implied by them; and that these premises might be selected so as to imply all true propositions, either directly or as the conclusions of implicatory chains emanating from them—like the *p*, *q*, and *r* of the paragraph above.   Such hopes are doomed. In the first place, no logically true proposition is *ipso facto* a proved proposition.   To be *proved,* a proposition must be the conclusion of an argument whose premises have been asserted, and where this is not the case, even the radiance of truth shining forth from the very structure of a logical proposition does not make it a *proved* truth.

A second reason why the maxim that not every proposition can be proved is valid even when the basic premises are supposed to be logical truths is that no logically true proposition could imply any factual proposition.   Logical truths, in fact, imply only other logical truths.   (A rigorous demonstration of this statement will be provided in Part Two, page 94.)   Any logical truth which could serve as a premise for factual truth would be conveying information about the world of facts; but we have already seen that logical propositions are wholly independent of facts.   No logically true proposition implies any proposition true only of the actual world simply because any logically true proposition is true of all possible worlds.   But if this is the case, a whole range of propositions—namely, those which are factual—will elude proof, no matter what logical truths we select as basic premises.   It follows that no description of our world can be deduced from a "self-evident" proposition whose "self-evidence" is alleged to be that of logic.

EXERCISES

A. Bearing in mind the definition of "argument" given at the beginning of this section, state which of the following sentences are arguments.   What is the conclusion of each?   In the case of each sentence which is *not* an argument, explain why it is not.

1. If winter comes, can spring be far behind?
2. If winter comes, spring cannot be far behind.
3. The arrival of winter is an argument for the imminence of spring.

4. Winter comes and spring is not far behind.
5. Since spring is far behind, winter has not yet come.
6. Spring cannot be far behind, in view of the fact that winter has come.
7. Winter is dreary; would that it were spring.
8. Because I hate winter, I ardently hope for spring.
9. I hope for warm weather, and warm weather occurs in the spring, therefore, I hope for spring.
10. Since robins nest only in the spring, and it is not spring, robins are not nesting.
11. I cannot answer you; for I have no idea what you mean.
12. How can I answer you when I have no idea what you mean?
13. Either I mean what you think I mean, or I do not mean what you think I mean.
14. Since I mean what I say, I say what I mean.
15. Since I like what I get, I get what I like.

B. The element of *inference* in an argument may be relatively strong or weak, depending upon the degree of assurance with which the speaker is able to assert the premises. Arrange the following arguments in the order of the strength of the inference involved, beginning with the strongest inference.

1. If Diggs cheated, and if all cheaters are dismissed, Diggs will be dismissed.
2. Diggs cheated; if all cheaters were dismissed, Diggs would be dismissed.
3. Since Diggs cheated, and since all cheaters are dismissed, Diggs will surely be dismissed.
4. Since it is likely that Diggs cheated, and since most cheaters are dismissed, there is a 50-50 chance that Diggs will be dismissed.
5. If Diggs had cheated, and if all cheaters were dismissed, Diggs would have been dismissed.

C. Perhaps one *could* prove everything, after all. Suppose we have proved r by asserting a q which implies r and we have also been able to prove q by asserting the premise p. Now suppose we find that r implies p. Since r has already been proved, p is thereby proved, and we have—it would seem—succeeded in proving *all* of our premises without having merely to *assume* any of them.

What is wrong with reasoning of this sort?

SUPPLEMENTARY READINGS

1. Ralph M. Eaton, *General Logic,* New York, Charles Scribner's Sons, 1931, Pt. I, Sec. 8.

2. John Cooley, *A Primer of Formal Logic,* New York, The Macmillan Company, 1942, Ch. 1.

6

Truth and Validity

Now that our vocabulary has been enlarged by the addition of the word "argument," let us return to logical and factual propositions. Liaison between Sections 4 and 5 is best established if we make a significant distinction between arguments which are logically true and those which are not. An argument which is itself a logical truth we shall call "a valid argument," and all others will be referred to as "invalid." Thus an argument is invalid if it is merely factually true, or either factually or logically false.

The following examples are valid arguments:

(6.1) Since all whales are mammals and no mammal is a fish, no whale is a fish.

(6.2) Since it is either raining or snowing and it is not raining, it is snowing.

The validity of these arguments may be demonstrated by observing that they are true independently of all facts or substitutions for inessential words. Thus 6.1 reduces to

(6.3) Since all ——— are ***** and no ***** is a /////, no ——— is a /////,

and the analysis of 6.2 yields the structure

(6.4) Since ——— or *****, and not ———, *****.

(Notice that the variables of 6.4, like those of 4.7 on page 18, are propositions as a whole. This is an example of what we shall later call "a propositional argument.")

On the other hand the argument "If Boggs is not in class, he is sick" is invalid. Its structure does not permit its assertion as logically true, even though this argument is plainly based upon what is quite possibly a fact. Although discussion throughout this book will be confined to valid arguments, we must recognize that certain invalid arguments are indispensable to the maintenance of human action. Science seeks to elicit implications which are true of our actual world, and the ordinary business of everyday life could not be transacted at all if we were not willing to base it on myriad arguments true only by virtue of facts. The investigation of the criteria in terms of which factually true arguments are justified or warranted is, however, the proper undertaking of inductive logic, and thus beyond the scope of this book.

Although a valid argument is logically true, each of its premises, as well as its conclusion, might be a factual proposition. At the end of Section 5 it was stated that a logical truth implies nothing but another logical truth. In other words, any argument, all of the premises of which are logically true, must have a logically true conclusion. This means that wherever the conclusion of the argument is factual, at least one of its premises must be factual, even when the argument as a whole is logically true, or valid. To illustrate this general principle we may examine the valid arguments 6.1 and 6.2.

Both arguments 6.1 and 6.2 have factual conclusions: "no whale is a fish" stands or falls on a zoological fact, and the truth or falsity of "it is snowing" depends upon a meteorological fact. Now the generalization we have just made will be borne out only if at least one premise of each of these propositions is factual. Inspection of 6.1 and 6.2 confirms the generalization: *all* of the premises involved are themselves factual propositions. It is obvious that both "it is either raining or snowing" and "it is not raining" are true or false depending on a local condition of our actual world;

and it is equally certain that "all whales are mammals" and "no mammal is a fish" are both dependent upon facts brought out in zoology. In summary, while 6.1 and 6.2 are both logically true, each consists wholly of factual propositions, except for the connecting logical words "and" and "since . . . , therefore. . . ."

Most useful valid arguments are like 6.1 and 6.2 in containing no proposition, in either premise or conclusion, which is not factual. Let us examine some additional examples which will, at the same time, bring out further characteristics of valid arguments.

(6.5) Since Boggs is not both a sophomore and a senior, and he is a senior, therefore he is not a sophomore.

(6.6) Since tomatoes are not both red and blue, and they are blue, therefore they are not red.

(6.7) Since silver is not both malleable and ductile, and it is ductile, therefore it is not malleable.

(6.8) Since wood is not both a liquid and a gas, and it is a gas, therefore it is not a liquid.

Every simple proposition occurring in each of these examples is factual; the student can verify this fact. Whoever does examine these arguments closely, however, will discover an apparently anomalous situation, for not all the factual propositions ingredient in 6.5 through 6.8 are true. This situation exists in spite of the fact that each of the arguments as a whole is a logical truth embodying the identical structure

(6.9) Since ———— is not both ***** and /////, and ———— is /////, therefore ———— is not *****.

Consider 6.6. The first premise "Tomatoes are not both red and blue" is clearly true. But the second premise and the conclusion are false. It is false that tomatoes are blue and false that they are not red.

The argument 6.7 contains two falsehoods: the first of its premises and its conclusion. And the conclusion of 6.8 is factually true even though the facts testify against the premise that wood is a gas. How are we to look at the relation between the logical truth of a valid argument and the factual truth or falsity of its premises?

The validity of a valid argument arises from its over-all structure. This structure overlays the separate factual propositions composing the argument, and in so doing, makes words that were essential to the separate propositions inessential to the whole. For instance, "silver" is essential to "silver is ductile"; replace it with "wood" and a truth turns into a falsehood. But "silver" is replaceable by any other word, throughout the whole of 6.7; here it is inessential. An argument is like a mosaic: each piece of the mosaic has a distinctive shape of its own, but it surrenders this shape when it enters the pattern as a whole. Juxtaposed squares become a rectangle by virtue of a shared edge. Similarly, juxtaposed facts become a logical truth by virtue of shared words.

Now if the essential words of a factual proposition can become inessential to the valid argument in which such a proposition occurs, it makes little difference to the argument whether its factual components are true or false. "Silver is ductile" is true; if we replace "silver" by "wood," the proposition becomes false, as we have just pointed out. But argument 6.7 sanctions this replacement; it sanctions any replacement for "silver" that we might choose. Thus 6.7 as a whole is explicitly indifferent to the truth or falsity of "silver is ductile."

The premises and conclusion of a valid argument may be variously true or false, with one important exception: *no valid argument can have all of its premises true, but its conclusion false.* Without this exception a central meaning of the relation of implication, which was pointed out in Section 5, would be violated. In that section it was stated that when any proposition is asserted to imply any other, the only situation which is ruled out is that in which the first is true but the second false. Thus to the extent that Boggs's absence from class implies that he is sick, he cannot be absent and at the same time not sick. This is an essential ingredient of the meaning of such implicatory words as "Since . . . , therefore. . . ." Thus we cannot suppose that a valid argument might have true premises but a false conclusion without unwittingly substituting some other word for the essential words "Since . . . , therefore. . . ." Where such a substitution is made, the argument loses its validity. (An *invalid* argument might, of course, have premises all true and conclusion true, premises not all true and conclusion true, premises all true and conclusion false, or premises not all true and conclusion false.)

Remembering the exception just noted, we may say that a *valid* argument might involve true premises and true conclusion, false premises and true conclusion, or false premises and false conclusion. This would seem to render valid arguments wholly irrelevant to human discourse. Far from being irrelevant, however, valid arguments are *necessary* to discourse because they are structures into which all facts fit. Not only do all facts fit into valid arguments, but more important, when appropriate facts are so fitted, new facts result. Because 6.9 is the structure of a logical truth, we may incorporate in it the independent facts "Boggs is not both a sophomore and a senior" and "Boggs is a senior" to obtain the new fact "Boggs is not a sophomore." If this fact does not surprise us, it is because the valid structure 6.9 is ingrained in the most essential processes of our thought; we always think in this fashion. In the succeeding parts we may find that some of the more complex structures yield surprising results. But we must not use novelty as a criterion for the value of logic. To be able to conclude that certain specific factual propositions, and not others, are implied by the facts at hand is fundamental to our every occasion of inquiry and communication. If we lacked this acumen, our world would be chaos. But a thought process so fundamental in this sense could scarcely be surprising to discover.

EXERCISES

A. Consider the following arguments.

    (a) All fish swim.
        All trout swim.
        Therefore, all trout are fish.

   (b) All fish swim.
        All trout are fish.
        Therefore, all trout swim.
   (c) All fish fly.
        All trout are fish.
        Therefore, all trout fly.
   (d) All fish fly.
        All trout fly.
        Therefore, all trout are fish.
   (e) All fish fly.
        All trout fly.
        Therefore, all fish are trout.
   (f) All fish fly.
        All robins are fish.
        Therefore, all robins fly.
   (g) All fish swim.
        All trout swim.
        Therefore, all fish are trout.

1. Which one of these arguments is *valid*, with premises *all true*, and conclusion *true?*
2. Which is *valid*, with premises *not all true*, and conclusion *true?*
3. Which is *valid*, with premises *not all true*, and conclusion *false?*
4. Which is *invalid*, with premises *all true*, and conclusion *true?*
5. Which is *invalid*, with premises *all true*, and conclusion *false?*
6. Which is *invalid*, with premises *not all true*, and conclusion *true?*
7. Which is *invalid*, with premises *not all true*, and conclusion *false?*
8. Why does the list contain no *valid* argument, with premises *all true* and conclusion *false?*
9. Are all *valid* arguments logically *true?*
10. Are all *invalid* arguments logically *false?* Explain.

B. With respect to the following arguments, answer questions 1-8 of Exercise A, above.

   (a) Nothing is both a solid and a liquid.
        Water at room temperature is not a solid.
        Therefore, water at room temperature is a liquid.
   (b) Nothing is both a solid and a liquid.
        Water at room temperature is a solid.

Therefore, water at room temperature is not a liquid.

(c) Nothing is both colorless and a liquid.
Water at room temperature is not colorless.
Therefore, water at room temperature is a liquid.

(d) Nothing is both a metal and a liquid.
Water at room temperature is liquid.
Therefore, water at room temperature is not a metal.

(e) Nothing is both a solid and a liquid.
Air is not a solid.
Therefore, air is a liquid.

(f) Nothing is both colorless and a gas.
Water at room temperature is not colorless.
Therefore, water at room temperature is a gas.

(g) Nothing is both a solid and a liquid.
Water at room temperature is a liquid.
Therefore, water at room temperature is not a solid.

SUPPLEMENTARY READING

Max Black, *Critical Thinking,* New York, Prentice-Hall, Inc., 2d ed. 1952, Ch. 2.

PART TWO

The Logic of Propositions

7

The Properties of Implication

In this part of our study we shall develop techniques for examining the validity of arguments in which propositions as a whole function as variables or inessential words. The example "Since ——— or *****, and not ———, therefore *****," used in Section 6, was an argument of this sort; we shall soon acknowledge a host of others. Meanwhile, it is desirable to outline the scope of this part by indicating what it excludes. The arguments specifically to be postponed until Part Three are all those to which single words rather than propositions as a whole are inessential. "If ——— is not both ***** and /////, and ——— is *****, then ——— is not ///// " may come to mind as an illustration of such arguments, because the blanks must be filled in by nouns or adjectives rather than by entire propositions. The type of argument, known as "the syllogism," is also of this type and so cannot be discussed until Part Three. The scope of the present chapter, then, may be called "the logic of propositions."

Since the logic of propositions is a distinct branch of logic, with problems not precisely those of that other branch in which nouns and adjectives are the inessential words, it is useful to adopt a set of symbols to stand particularly for propositions when they are inessential to a logical truth. These symbols are the letters p, q, r, and s. We shall henceforth employ them wherever they are relevant, rather than blanks. Later on, other letters will be

41

introduced to represent variables of the remaining types, so that
blanks will drop out altogether.   The argument "Since ———— or
*****, and not ————, therefore *****," when recast in our new
symbolism, becomes simply "Since p or q, and not p, therefore q."
Here p and q are the variables, and "If . . . then . . . ," "or,"
"and," and "not" are the essential words or logical constants.

There are several kinds of propositional arguments, and in
connection with each of these kinds there are particular problems
which may be solved by means of techniques to be explained in
the sections that follow.   First, however, it is desirable to amplify
the remarks about implication which occurred in Section 5 (page
25).   For the successful analysis of particular kinds of propositional arguments depends to a considerable extent upon our having
as clear an understanding as we can of the element of implication
which all valid arguments have in common.

The idea of implication is one of the two or three most important notions required for the study of logic.   But like several
other essential ideas (including that of logic itself) implication
cannot be defined in terms of any concept more familiar than itself
—and even when less familiar concepts are employed, any definition of implication seems arbitrary.   At best we can develop
certain ramifications of implication, but only on the assumption
that everyone already possesses that central idea the consequences
of which are to be discussed.

In general, when one proposition, say, p, implies another, which
we may represent as q, the significance of the implication over and
above the meanings of p and q in themselves is that p is a *sufficient
condition* for q.   For "p implies q" rules out the possibility that p
might be true while q is false.   Thus the truth of p is sufficient to
guarantee the truth of q.   Consider, for example,

(7.1) If Boggs is a Communist, he advocates the overthrow of
      bourgeois government.

This proposition is not concerned to establish either that Boggs *is*
a Communist or that Boggs actually does have revolutionary in-

tentions.   Either of these statements could lead to a libel suit if falsely asserted, whereas 7.1 as a whole would be legally innocuous even when both of its components were false.   Thus the primary significance of 7.1 is the connection it alleges to hold between these two components.   *If* Boggs is a Communist, this fact is *sufficient* to establish his revolutionary intentions; for Boggs could not *be* a Communist *without* advocating the overthrow of bourgeois government.   Boggs's Communism is thus a sufficient condition for his advocacy of force.

We are now ready to continue our development of a system of symbolism and technical terminology.   In the first place, "p implies q" may be conveniently written "$p \rightarrow q$."   This symbolic expression may be read not only as "p implies q," but also as "if p, then q" or as "p only if q."   Care should be exercised, however, to avoid the supposition that "$p \rightarrow q$" means "p *if* q."   For "p *if* q" is no more than a grammatical inversion of "if q, then p," and, as both the foregoing discussion and the following analysis should make clear, "*if q, then p*" does not have at all the same meaning as "$p \rightarrow q$" or "if p, then q."

There are many words and phrases in colloquial English which express implication.   Those associated with the premises and conclusion of an argument have already been mentioned, for example, "since . . . , therefore . . . ," "for," and "so."   In addition there are phrases such as "if . . . , then . . ." which convey no explicit ingredient of inference.   Thus "provided that p, q" and "in case p, q" both mean "$p \rightarrow q$."   Some caution should be observed with "p *unless* q."   This, essentially, means "p if not q," or, in other words, "if not q, then p."   But it occasionally has an additional overtone: "I will lend you this book unless you intend to underline it" clearly means at least "If you do not intend to underline this book, I will lend it to you."   However, it also seems to mean "If you intend to underline this book, I will not lend it to you."   And, as the next few pages will show, these two meanings are by no means equivalent.

Whenever $p \rightarrow q$, p is said to be the *antecedent,* and q, the *con-*

sequent. The antecedent of a valid argument is thus its set of premises, and the consequent of such an argument is its conclusion. All that any proposition containing implication alleges is that its antecedent cannot be true while its consequent is false. It ascribes neither truth nor falsehood to the antecedent or consequent alone. Thus whenever $p \to q$, q must be true if p is true, but if p is false, q may be either true or false. Consider the preceding example (7.1), which we can now phrase as "Boggs is a Communist $\to$ Boggs advocates revolution." This tells us only that Boggs cannot be a Communist without advocating revolution; if he should turn out *not* to be a Communist, then he may not advocate revolution at all, or may advocate it for other reasons.

Any proposition containing implication is said to be *conditional* or *hypothetical.* The phrase "a conditional proposition" is often shortened to "a conditional," just as a periodical publication is usually called "a periodical." All valid arguments are thus conditional propositions, but the phrase "conditional argument" is, as we shall see, reserved for those arguments which have at least one conditional premise. We have already suggested one motive for this nomenclature; the antecedent of a conditional proposition is a *sufficient condition* for the consequent. Another motive is that the consequent is a *necessary condition* for the antecedent; the consequent is necessary in the sense that when it fails, the antecedent must fail, too. Thus the three following propositions are precisely equivalent:

Boggs is a registered voter $\to$ Boggs is a citizen of the United States.

Boggs's being a registered voter is a sufficient condition for his citizenship in the United States (that is, is sufficent to insure that he is a citizen).

Boggs's citizenship in the United States is a necessary condition for his being a registered voter.

For every conditional proposition such as "$p \to q$," there are three important related propositions: the *converse* "$q \to p$," the *contrapositive* "not $q \to$ not p," and the *contradictory* "not ($p \to$

q)," where the parentheses indicate that the "not" applies to "$p \rightarrow q$" as a whole, and not just to p. Let us consider these in turn.

The *converse* of a conditional is *independent* of it; when a given conditional is true, its converse may be true or may, on the other hand, be false. Thus, "Today is Monday $\rightarrow$ tomorrow is Tuesday" and its converse, "Tomorrow is Tuesday $\rightarrow$ today is Monday" happen both to be true, but, while "Boggs is a Vermonter $\rightarrow$ Boggs is a New Englander" is true, "Boggs is a New Englander $\rightarrow$ Boggs is a Vermonter" is definitely false.

The confusion of a conditional with its converse is probably the source of more erroneous reasoning than all the other possible fallacies put together. It is an error, for example, to suppose that just because a scientific theory implies that certain events will be observed, it follows that the observation of these events implies the truth of the theory. The proposition "The theory of evolution is true $\rightarrow$ fossils of extinct species will be found" is itself certainly true, but it cannot validly be argued from this proposition that the discovery of the appropriate fossils proves the truth of the theory of evolution, with all of its ramifications. In the nineteenth century theologians asserted that the fossils actually discovered were put there by God to test men's faith; and *this* follows from the true conditional in question with precisely the same validity as does the claim that Evolution is true.

The *contrapositive* of any conditional is always exactly equivalent to it; that is, when "$p \rightarrow q$" is true, "not $q \rightarrow$ not p" is true, and when "$p \rightarrow q$" is false, "not $q \rightarrow$ not p" is false. This relationship between a conditional and its contrapositive arises from the fact that "$p \rightarrow q$" means only "it cannot be the case that p is true while q is false"; so that *if* q is false, p must likewise be false. But this is simply to say, "not $q \rightarrow$ not p."

Consider again, for example, "Boggs is a Communist $\rightarrow$ Boggs advocates revolution." This means no more than that Boggs cannot be a Communist without advocating revolution. Thus if he does *not* advocate revolution, he cannot be a Communist.

It seems best to treat the *contradictory* of "$p \rightarrow q$" as a special case of contradictories in general; the notion of a contradictory is essential to logical inquiry, and applies to any proposition whatsoever, whether it is conditional or not. The contradictory of a proposition, say, *p,* is a proposition related to it in such a way that, of *p* and its contradictory, one must be true and the other false; it is impossible for both to be true at the same time and in the same respect. The contradictory of "it is raining" is "it is not raining"; in general, where *p* is taken as a whole without consideration for such parts as it may have, its contradictory is "not *p.*" The contradictory of a proposition must be sharply distinguished from its *contraries,* that is, those propositions which cannot be true when the given proposition is true but may well be false when it is false. "All tomatoes are red," for example, is contradicted only by "Some tomatoes are not red." Plausible as it may seem, "No tomatoes are red" does not contradict "All tomatoes are red," since it is possible for both of these propositions to be false. Indeed, both are false; some tomatoes are red, and some are not. These two last propositions are therefore only contraries of one another; they are not contradictories.

Colloquial English makes available a variety of ways to express the contradictory of a proposition. Where *p* is the proposition in question, its contradictory might be rendered as "not *p,*" "it is not the case that *p,*" "it is false that *p,*" or "*p* is false." In addition, the word "contradictory" itself has several equivalents, including "denial" and "negation." This last word is often used in the phrasing of a centrally important law of logic, known as the "Law of Double Negation," according to which *the negation of the negation of a proposition is the proposition* itself. Thus "not not *p*" means simply "*p.*"

By the definition of "contradictory" just given, "$p \rightarrow q$" has "not $(p \rightarrow q)$" as its contradictory. This does not take into consideration, however, the fact that "$p \rightarrow q$" as a whole is a complex proposition. In such cases it is often possible to transform the proposition in such a way that the "not" is absorbed into its internal structure. In order to transform "not $(p \rightarrow q)$" into a more useful contradictory, we have only to reflect upon the meaning of "$p \rightarrow q$"; namely, that it is false that p holds while q fails; more simply, it is false that p but not q.

Another version of the contradictory of "$p \rightarrow q$," then, is "p but not q." Note that while the converse and the contrapositive of any conditional proposition are themselves conditionals, the contradictory of a conditional proposition is not a conditional. The peculiar form which "p but not q" does have will be analyzed later.

Any conditional has an indefinite number of contraries, but it would serve no present purpose to exemplify them here. The notion of a contrary becomes important only in Part Three, where we shall be dealing with the nonpropositional parts of simple propositions. We possess now a technical vocabulary which is at least adequate for dealing with conditional arguments. To these we shall now proceed.

EXERCISES

A. Which of the following propositions means the same as "Suggs took the subway → he arrived on time"?

1. If Suggs did not take the subway, he did not arrive on time.
2. Suggs did not arrive on time if he did not take the subway.
3. Suggs arrived on time unless he did not take the subway.
4. Suggs took the subway unless he did not arrive on time.
5. Suggs did not arrive on time only if he did not take the subway.
6. Suggs took the subway but arrived on time.
7. It is not the case that Suggs took the subway but did not arrive on time.
8. It is not the case that Suggs arrived on time but did not take the subway.
9. Suggs arrived on time provided that he took the subway.
10. Suggs took the subway only if he arrived on time.
11. If Suggs arrived on time, he took the subway.
12. If Suggs took the subway, he arrived on time.
13. Suggs arrived on time if he took the subway.
14. Suggs arrived on time only if he did not take the subway.
15. In case Suggs did not arrive on time, he did not take the subway.

(*Suggestion:* Begin by symbolizing each proposition, using "S" for "Suggs took the subway" and "A" for "He arrived on time." This will clarify the form of the proposition.)

B. What are the converse, contrapositive, and contradictory of each of the following conditional propositions?

1. If it is raining, Diggs will get wet.
2. The grass will grow only if it rains.
3. The grass will grow if it rains.
4. If the length of a rectangle is doubled, then its area is doubled.
5. If I am fated to pass, then I am not fated to fail.
6. I am fated to pass, unless I am fated to fail.
7. Unless you agree to return the book, I will not lend it to you.
8. If some tomatoes are vegetables, then some vegetables are to-matoes.
9. If x is greater than y, then y is less than x.
10. State will win, provided that Boggs does not pitch.

C. Are the contradictories of propositions 4, 8, and 9, above, ever true? What does this mean with respect to the status of these conditionals as logical or factual? In general, is the contradictory of a logical proposition ever conceivable?

SUPPLEMENTARY READINGS

1. Morris R. Cohen and Ernest Nagel, *An Introduction to Logic and Scientific Method,* New York, Harcourt, Brace and Company, 1934, Ch. I, Sec. 3.

2. C. I. Lewis and C. H. Langford, *Symbolic Logic,* New York, The Century Co., 1932, Ch. 8. (Most elementary students will find this book somewhat too technical for their purposes.)

8

Conditional Arguments

A conditional argument may be defined as a propositional argument at least one premise of which is a conditional. The two following arguments, for example, are both conditional arguments:

(8.1) If Boggs died, his life insurance was paid; Boggs died, so his life insurance was paid.

(8.2) If Boggs died, his life insurance was paid, and if his life insurance was paid, his widow is well off; therefore, if Boggs died, his widow is well off.

The distinctive feature of 8.1, as well as of 8.2, by virtue of which each is identified as a conditional argument, is the essential occurrence of "If . . . then . . ." within the premises. "If . . . then . . ." is a word for implication; hitherto (in Section 5) we have considered only the cases of implication in which it relates the *premises* of an argument to its *conclusion*. Now, however, we are in a position to see that such a case of implication is only a special case of implication in general.

Both 8.1 and 8.2 happen to be valid arguments. Their validity is established by the possibility of analyzing them into the respective structures

(8.3) If p, then q; p, so q

(8.4) If p, then q, and if q, then r; therefore, if p, then r

Here p, q, and r are genuine variables of the sort occurring within the logic of propositions; each may be replaced by any proposition whatsoever (but not by any noun or adjective) without altering the status of 8.3 or 8.4 as logically true.

It is possible to express, in terms of the arrow we are using to symbolize implication, both the implication contained within the premises of 8.3 and 8.4, and that which connects the respective sets of premises taken together with the respective conclusions. Thus, 8.4 becomes

(8.5) $[(p \rightarrow q) \text{ and } (q \rightarrow r)] \rightarrow (p \rightarrow r)$

Here the brackets and parentheses indicate how the constituent propositions of 8.5 are to be regarded as grouped together; the use of such brackets and parentheses will be explained more fully in Section 9 (page 64) where symbolism like that of 8.5 will be employed.   For the moment, however, the implication between the premises and conclusions of an argument is more conveniently expressed by the use of a horizontal line.   Thus in this section we shall represent 8.3 as

(8.6) $p \rightarrow q$

$$\frac{p}{q}$$

and 8.4 as

(8.7) $p \rightarrow q$

$$\frac{q \rightarrow r}{p \rightarrow r}$$

It should be borne in mind that although the implication occurring within the premises of a conditional argument is not symbolized in the same way as is the implication which binds the premises of an argument to its conclusion, the significance of implication is exactly the same in both cases.   Whether we write "$p \rightarrow q$" or $\dfrac{\text{``}p\text{,''}}{q}$ we intend that q be dependent on p in the sense that *p* is a sufficient condition for *q*, and we rule out the possibility that *p* is true while *q* is false. In neither case, furthermore, do we take any responsibility for the truth or falsity of *p* or *q* alone. The only reason for using two different symbols for implication is that we want to distinguish between its occurrences as the relation between the premises and conclusion of a valid argument and its other occurrences within the premises or conclusion of such an argument.

The argument 8.6 above is, as we have seen, valid, because its truth is independent of any fact, situation, circumstance, or state of affairs. In particular, it states only that when the antecedent of a true conditional is true, its consequent must be true; and this follows from the very meaning of "implication." This way of arguing is often called *modus ponens* (Latin for "way of assertion"), and reflects the fact that the antecedent is asserted.

Another valid form of argument is

$$(8.8) \quad p \rightarrow q$$
$$\underline{\quad \text{not } q \quad}$$
$$\text{not } p$$

This form expresses the equivalence of "$p \rightarrow q$" and its contrapositive: if *q* fails, then *p* must likewise fail. The Latin expression for this argumentative technique is *modus tollens,* or "way of denial"; it takes account of the fact that the consequent of the conditional is denied.

To the conditional "If Russia invades Western Europe, the United States will go to war" we may add the premise "Russia invades Western Europe" and argue by *modus ponens* to the conclusion "The United States will go to war"; alternatively, the addition of the premise "The United States will not go to war" leads, by *modus tollens,* to "Russia does not invade Western Europe." But these alternatives exhaust the possibilities. Anyone who, adding the premise "Russia does not invade Western Europe," draws the conclusion "The United States will not go to war," is arguing invalidly; in particular, he is committing the *fallacy of denying the antecedent.* His argument is fallacious because the conditional premise at hand does not rule out the possibility that the United States might go to war for other reasons; for example, Russia might invade the Philippines. Similarly, to apply the premise "The United States will go to war" and conclude therefrom that Russia invades Western Europe is to commit a fallacy, in this case the *fallacy of asserting the consequent.* Once again, the premise applied does not rule out the possibility of an American declaration of war motivated by other events. This latter fallacy is a form of the common confusion previously noted between a proposition and its converse (see page 45).

The two fallacies just mentioned are, in general, the invalid arguments

$$(8.9) \quad p \to q$$
$$\underline{\text{not } p}$$
$$\text{not } q$$

and

$$(8.10) \quad p \to q$$
$$\underline{q}$$
$$p$$

The first denies the antecedent, and the second asserts the consequent. Both 8.9 and 8.10 are traps into which the most careful arguers sometimes fall; it is important to be constantly on the look-out for them.

Let us elaborate on another type of conditional argument mentioned above (page 49). This is the type represented by 8.7; namely,

$$p \to q$$
$$\underline{q \to r}$$
$$p \to r$$

Any argument of this sort will be called a *chain argument.* Some authors prefer the terminology "Pure Hypothetical Syllogism," but this reflects an ancient classification of arguments, the usefulness of which is no longer unquestionable. The distinguishing feature of a chain argument is that all of its premises and its conclusion are conditional propositions. The function of such an argument is to eliminate a simple proposition, such as the q in 8.6 which appears in one premise as the antecedent and the other as the consequent. In general, a chain argument is valid when the proposition eliminated does occur once as an antecedent and once as a consequent, and when the antecedent of the conclusion was the antecedent of a premise and the consequent of the conclusion was the consequent of a premise. Argument 8.2 (page 49) satisfies these requirements and is valid, as is

(8.11) The thermometer reads five below → my car won't start.
My car won't start → I won't get to class on time.
_____
The thermometer reads five below → I won't get to class on time.

On the other hand, to violate as do the following examples, any of the stipulations just given, leads to a fallacy.

(8.12) The thermometer reads five below → my car won't start.
I won't get to class on time → my car won't start.
_____
The thermometer reads five below → I won't get to class on time.

(8.13) The thermometer reads five below → my car won't start.
My car won't start → I won't get to class on time.
_____
I won't get to class on time → the thermometer reads five below.

That these arguments are fallacious is obvious; the alleged conclusions are by no means implied by the premises in question. Technically, their invalidity arises from the fact that in 8.12, "my car won't start" occurs as a consequent twice but never as an antecedent, and in 8.13 the antecedent of the conclusion did not occur in the premises as an antecedent, nor did its consequent occur there as a consequent.

A chain argument must have at least two premises, but may

have any number greater than two. In general, we may represent the structure of a valid chain argument as follows:

(8.14) $p \rightarrow q$

      .   .   .

$$\frac{y \rightarrow z}{p \rightarrow z}$$

Here it is understood that the rules regarding the propositions successively eliminated, as well as those governing the order of propositions in the conclusion, are strictly observed.

Many cases are possible in which a valid chain argument may seem invalid because its premises have been transposed or the contrapositive has been substituted for one or more of them. The following argument, for instance, is impeccable:

(8.15)   If I can buy a ticket to New York, I shall go to New York.
        If I do not leave on Friday, I shall not go to New York.
        If you pay me what you owe me, I can buy a ticket to New York.

        If you pay me what you owe me, I shall leave on Friday.

To test the validity of 8.15, let us first throw it into symbolic form:

(8.16) $B \rightarrow G$
        not $L \rightarrow$ not G
        $\dfrac{P \rightarrow B}{P \rightarrow L}$

Here B represents "I can buy a ticket to New York," G stands for "I shall go to New York," L signifies "I shall leave on Friday," and P symbolizes "You pay me what you owe me." The first step in reducing this argument to the standard form of 8.14 is to replace premises with their contrapositives until each simple proposition eliminated by the conclusion occurs once as an antecedent and once as a consequent; where this is not possible, the argument may be rejected at once as invalid. Only one such operation is necessary for 8.16; the substitution for the second premise of its contrapositive yields

(8.17) $B \rightarrow G$
$\quad\quad G \rightarrow L$
$\quad\quad P \rightarrow B$
$\quad\quad \overline{P \rightarrow L}$

Now we must transpose the premises in such a way that the antecedent of the first is the antecedent of the conclusion and the consequent of the last is the consequent of the conclusion. Again, if this procedure is impossible, the argument is invalid. In the case of 8.17 we have only to transfer the premise "$P \rightarrow B$" from the last position to the first, obtaining

(8.18) $P \rightarrow B$
$\quad\quad B \rightarrow G$
$\quad\quad G \rightarrow L$
$\quad\quad \overline{P \rightarrow L}$

Since 8.18 exhibits precisely the structure of 8.14, 8.18 is valid.

Occasionally, the consequent of the last premise of a chain argument is the contradictory of the antecedent of the first premise. When this is true, the conclusion will be of the form "$p \rightarrow$ not p." To the beginning student of logic, the notion of a proposition which implies its own contradictory will seem strange; must not the argument from which such a conclusion follows be invalid? In order to answer this question, we shall consider a concrete example. A student planning his schedule might argue thus:

(8.19) If I am free on Monday at ten, I will take Modern Poetry.
$\quad\quad$ If I take Modern Poetry, I will not be free on Monday at ten.
$\quad\quad$ If I am free on Monday at ten, I will not be free on Monday at ten.

This may sound like a ridiculous bit of sophistry, but it is a perfectly valid argument. It proves, simply, that the student will not, under any circumstances, be free on Monday at ten, for all that its conclusion asserts is that the possibility that this hour might be free while not being not free is ruled out. The possibility that the hour is free is ruled out, or the hour is simply not free. In general, when $p \rightarrow$ not p, all that is excluded is the possibility that p is true when "not p" is false, or, equivalently, the possibility that p is true.   Thus from "$p \rightarrow$ not p" we may always conclude "not p." This is the simplest form of the conditional argument; it has only one premise.   We may represent it as follows:

(8.20) $p \rightarrow$ not p

not p

Any argument having the form of 8.20 is known as an *indirect proof*.   Proofs of this sort are common in mathematics and the sciences; the student will recall that many theorems in plane geometry are proved by assuming the contradictory of the theorem and showing that this implies its *own* contradictory, whence the theorem in question follows.   Detective stories make liberal use of indirect proof; the following argument is typical

(8.21) If Boggs committed the murder, he arrived on the 8:28.
        If he arrived on the 8:28, he left his home on the 8:04.
        If he left his home on the 8:04, he had no opportunity to procure the weapon.
        If he had no opportunity to procure the weapon, he did not commit the murder.

        If Boggs committed the murder, he did not commit the murder.

From the conclusion of 8.21 it follows that Boggs did not commit the murder.   But we need not concentrate on crime to find many instances of indirect proof.   We devise them every day.   Can the houseparty dance be held out-of-doors?   Did one's roommate go home?   One may often argue best to satisfactory replies to such questions if one shows that a certain hypothesis is ruled out because it implies its own contradictory.

A form of argumentation closely related to indirect proof is *reductio ad absurdum*.   This type of argument consists in the demonstration that a certain proposition implies both another proposition and the contradictory of that proposition; stated symbolically,

(8.22) $p \to q$ and $p \to$ not q

This is tantamount to indirect proof because we may arrange these two conditionals as the premises of an argument:

(8.23) $p \to$ not q

  $p \to q$

Taking the contrapositive of the second premise, we have

(8.24) $p \to$ not q

  not $q \to$ not p

  ————————

  $p \to$ not p

Here the proposition eliminated by the conclusion is "not *q*." The conclusion itself permits the further conclusion, "not *p*." A famous instance of *reductio ad absurdum* is Euclid's proof that there is no highest prime number. Others, from mathematics, the sciences, and everyday life, will occur to the reader.

Modus ponens, modus tollens, the chain argument, indirect proof, and *reductio ad absurdum,* exhaust the common forms of the conditional argument. Something remains to be said about the *dilemma,* the premises of which are partly conditional. But logical words other than those for implication also occur essentially in the premises of a dilemma; Section 9 will be devoted to arguments involving these other words.

EXERCISE

Symbolize each of the following arguments, using the symbols suggested. B. Identify the argument. C. State whether it is valid.

Sample: If it is raining, Diggs is wet. But it is raining. Therefore, Diggs is wet.   (R,D)
  Ans. A. R → D   B. Modus ponens.   C. Valid.

    R

    ———

    D

  1. If it is raining, Diggs is wet. But Diggs *is* wet. Therefore, it is raining.   (R,D)

2. If it is raining, Diggs is wet. But Diggs is not wet. Therefore, it is not raining. (R,D)

3. If Meggs is studying theology, he takes Greek. But he does not take Greek. So he is not studying theology. (T,G)

4. Meggs can take Greek only if he has had Latin. Since he cannot take Greek, it follows that he has not had Latin. (G,L)

5. Meggs can take Greek if he has had Latin. Since he cannot take Greek, it follows that he has not had Latin. (G,L)

6. In case it rained, the game was to be called. Since the game *was* called, it must have rained. (R,C)

7. If the knob is turned, the closet door will swing open, and if the closet door swings open, the hats will fall from the hooks. Therefore, if the knob is turned, the hats will fall from the hooks. (K,C,H)

8. If the knob is turned, the closet door will swing open, and if the knob is turned, my wife will be suspicious. Therefore, if the closet door swings open, my wife will be suspicious. (K,C,S)

9. I shall hear from Boggs today provided that he wrote Thursday. Since he did write Thursday, it follows that I shall hear from him today. (H,W)

10. I'll go to the movies only if I can get my work done. But I can get my work done. So I'll go to the movies. (M,W)

11. Unless a quiz is announced, Suggs does not come to class. Suggs is in class today. Therefore, a quiz must have been announced. (Q,S)

12. If there is a good movie, Suggs does not study. Suggs is studying. Therefore, no good movie is in town. (M,S)

13. In case there is not a party, Suggs leaves town. But this weekend there is no party. It follows that Suggs will leave town. (P,S)

14. In case there is not a party, Suggs leaves town. Suggs is nowhere to be found. Thus there is no party. (P,S)

15. If prices are high, it is not a favorable time to buy.
    If prices are not high, the product is not in demand.
    _____
    If the product is not in demand, it is a favorable time to buy.
    (H,F,D)

16. The wheel turns only if the ratchet is not engaged.
    If the lever is not down, the ratchet is engaged.
    _____
    If the wheel turns, the lever is down. (W,R,L)

17. Diggs's death is a necessary condition for the payment of his life insurance. Since Diggs has died, his life insurance has been paid. (D,P)

18. If the Theory of Evolution is true, there will be fossils of extinct forms. If the account of Creation in the Book of Genesis is true, there will not be fossils of extinct forms. Thus, if the account of Creation in the Book of Genesis is true, the Theory of Evolution is false. (E,F,G)

19. The acceleration of a falling body is independent of its weight only if two cannon balls of unequal weight strike the ground simultaneously after having been released simultaneously. Since this experiment has been successfully performed, the conclusion that the acceleration of a falling body *is* independent of its weight may be considered established. (I,S)

20. Two different triangles having corresponding sides equal can be constructed on the same base only if the triangles are not different. It follows that two different triangles with corresponding sides equal cannot be constructed on the same base. (T) (See Euclid, Bk. I, Prop. VII)

21. Meggs is unapproachable unless Diggs is away, but Diggs is away only if business has fallen off. Therefore, if business has fallen off, Meggs is approachable. (M,D,B)

22. If the class meets today, the instructor must be sick. But if the instructor is sick, the class cannot very well meet today. Hence, the class does not meet today. (C,S)

23. If Boggs is from Georgia, he is from the South; and if Boggs is not from the East, he is not from Georgia. Therefore, Boggs is not from the South unless he is from the East. (G,S,E)

24. In case this object is iron, it will sink in water. For it is iron only if it is denser than water; and if it is denser than water, it will sink in water. (I,S,D)

25. Assuming that *if x is greater than y, then y is not greater than x,* it can easily be shown that *x* is not greater than itself. For if *x is* greater than *x*, then, by the assumption just stated, *x* is *not* greater than *x*. From this it follows simply that *x* is not greater than *x*. (G)

26. Unless Boggs cheated, he did not get all the answers right. If Boggs cheated, Suggs will report him.

If Boggs got all the answers right, Suggs will report him. (B,A,S)

27. If infinity is a number, then infinity + 1 is a distinct number.
    If infinity is a number, then infinity + 1 is not a distinct number.

    Infinity is not a number.   (I,D)
28. If the valve is turned, water flows into the tank.
    If the valve is not turned, Meggs is asleep on the job.

    If Meggs is asleep on the job, water does not flow into the tank.
    (V,W,M)
29. If Homer composed the Odyssey, he lived 200 years before the
    Iliad was written.
    Homer did not compose the Iliad if he lived 200 years before
    it was written.

    If Homer composed the Iliad, he did not compose the Odyssey.
    (O,L,I)
30. It will snow if the barometer drops.
    It is not the case that I will ski but at the same time not break
    my leg.
    Provided that it snows, I will ski.

    If the barometer drops, I will break my leg.   (Sn,B,Sk,L)
31. If Diggs is human, he is a biped.
    If Diggs is not rational, he is not human.

    If Diggs is rational, he is a biped.   (H,B,R)
32. If evil exists, God must have created it.
    If evil exists, God could not have created it.

    Evil does not exist.   (E,G)
33. If Boggs wrote this book, then Meggs was not the author.   But
    Meggs is lying unless he is the author.   And he will not be
    dismissed only if he is not lying.   If he is dismissed, he will
    have to find another position.   Therefore, if Boggs wrote this
    book, then Meggs will have to find another position.
    (Use B for "Boggs wrote this book," M for "Meggs was the
    author," L for "Meggs is lying," D for "Meggs will be dis-
    missed," F for "Meggs will have to find another position.")

SUPPLEMENTARY READINGS

1. Monroe C. Beardsley, *Practical Logic,* New York, Prentice-Hall,
Inc., 1950, Ch. 11.

2. Max Black, *Critical Thinking,* New York, Prentice-Hall, Inc., 2d
ed., 1952, Ch. 4.

9

Other Forms of Propositional Arguments

Now that we have examined several forms of the conditional argument with considerable care, we can afford to accelerate our pace in studying arguments whose premises contain words other than "→." The feeling for the structure of a valid argument should now be a familiar one, and we possess a fairly extensive technical vocabulary, the usefulness of which will be in evidence throughout the material to follow. To avoid needless reiteration in this section, the structure of those valid arguments in the logic of propositions in which implication does not occur essentially in the premises will merely be listed. A subsidiary aim of this section is to introduce some important new symbolism.

It has already been pointed out that from the premises

> It is either raining or snowing

and

> It is not raining

the conclusion

> It is snowing

follows. This argument, in which "or" rather than "→" is essential to the first premise, typifies those with which we shall be dealing in this section. Let us examine the argument more closely. Its structure is as follows:

(9.1) p or q

      not p

      q

This is a valid argument; its truth is independent of any proposition substituted for p or q.   Let us now inquire whether there are any other valid forms having "p or q" as a premise.   Surely, if 9.1 is valid,

(9.2) p or q

      not q

      p

has equal cogency.   This reversal is sanctioned by the fact that order is wholly irrelevant to two propositions connected by "or"; "q or p" means precisely "p or q."   Therefore, 9.2 is valid.

Doubts, however, arise with regard to the validity of the following form:

(9.3) p or q

      p

      not q

If the first premise in 9.3 is "Boggs is male or Boggs is female," the conclusion, "Boggs is not female" certainly follows when the second premise, "Boggs is male" is supplied.   But from the premises

Boggs is an Elk or Boggs is a Mason

and

Boggs is an Elk

it does not follow that Boggs is not a Mason; he might be both an Elk and a Mason.   Finally, in the case of

It is either raining or snowing
It is raining

we shall not know at all how to conclude; the possibility of a conclusion depends upon the possibility of simultaneous rain and snow, and from the expression, "It is either raining or snowing," taken in isolation, we cannot tell whether this possibility is envisaged by the speaker. The argument is valid only if it is not considered possible for rain and snow to fall at the same time.

If the validity of an argument of this sort depends on what the arguer means, let us make the meaning explicit. In particular, let us adopt a special symbol for the sort of "or" that connects two propositions both of which might be true, for example, "Boggs is an Elk" and "Boggs is a Mason." The symbol usually adopted for this purpose is "v," the initial letter of the Latin conjunction *vel*. The complex proposition "p v q" is said to exhibit the *inclusive "or"* which joins two propositions both of which may be true. "Boggs is male or Boggs is female," on the other hand, exhibits an *exclusive "or."*

Just as any proposition containing "→" is called a conditional, so any proposition in which "v" occurs may be referred to as an *alternation*. An *alternative argument* is one having at least one premise which is an alternation. In the symbolism we have just adopted, the two valid forms of alternative arguments are

(9.4) p v q

not p
___
q

(9.5) p v q

not q
___
p

On the present interpretation of "or," two forms become invalid; namely, those which falsely assume that v is exclusive. These are

(9.6) p v q

p
___
not q

(9.7) p v q

q
___
not p

The fallacy committed in 9.6 and 9.7 will receive the provisional classification *fallacy of alternation;* soon we are to see that this fallacy is precisely the same as either asserting the consequent or denying the antecedent in a conditional argument.   The fallacy of alternation is exemplified by the argument

> Tito is a Communist v Tito sympathizes with the West.
> Tito is a Communist.
> _____
> Tito does not sympathize with the West.

This is fallacious simply because the first premise does not necessarily presuppose the exclusiveness of the two alternatives.

We shall find it useful to inquire under what conditions an alternation is false.   And the very meaning of "v" provides us with requisite information; " *p* v *q*" *fails only when p and q are both false.*   It is for precisely this reason that the addition of the premise "not *p*" yields the conclusion *q*; for if *p* fails, then "*p* v *q*" can be true only on the condition that *q* is true.

We are for the moment neglecting to symbolize the exclusive "or."   There are several reasons for this negligence.   One is that in the symbolic method to be developed in the next section, it is simpler to deal with "v" than with the exclusive "or."   Another is that before long we shall find a neat way of expressing this notion in other terms, so that a distinct symbol is gratuitous.

Many arguments involve premises internally connected by the essential word "and."   Let us call such arguments *conjunctive,* and symbolize "and" by the ampersand "&."   This is also a propitious opportunity for introducing a symbol for "not"; our structures are now capable of being thrown wholly into symbolic form. For "not," we shall use the hyphen "-," prefixing this symbol to any proposition to form its contradictory.   "*p* & -*q*" thus means "*p* and not *q*"; "-*p* v -*q*" means "not *p* or not *q*"; "-(*p* → *q*)" means the contradictory of "*p* → *q*."   As in this last case, parentheses must be used to indicate the grouping of propositions over which "-" operates, except when only a single proposition is being denied (for example, -*p*).   Thus, "*p* & -(*q* v *r*)" means "*p* and the contradictory of q v r"; this should not be confused with "p & $(-q$ v $r)$."

Several words in English have the same basic logical meaning as "and"; these include "but," "while," and "although." Shades of rhetorical significance differentiate these words, but for logical purposes, they are all replaceable by "&." Thus "p but not q," which was previously made out to be the contradictory of "$p \rightarrow q$," may be written "p & $-q$."

Two propositions connected by "&" are said to be *conjoined*, or to form a *conjunct* or *conjunction;* one may argue from any conjunct to either of the propositions conjoined. The following is an example:

(9.8) It is noon & I am hungry.

It is noon.

Such a conjunctive argument is, however, so trivial that we shall not take the trouble to record its simple structure. A conjunctive argument is, in general, useful only when one of its premises is the *denial* of a conjunct. The following argument illustrates this point:

(9.9) -(Boggs is a Democrat & Boggs is a Republican).
Boggs is a Democrat.

-Boggs is a Republican.

The logical structure of an argument of this sort may be either

(9.10) -(p & q)   or   -(p & q)
$\quad\quad\;\; p$ q

$\quad\quad\; -q$ $-p$

A negative conclusion is thus enforced by an added affirmative premise. The converse of this is not, however, valid; the *fallacy of conjunction* is committed by anyone who argues

(9.11) -(Boggs is a Democrat & Boggs is a Republican).
-Boggs is a Democrat.

Boggs is a Republican.

since it is conceivable that Boggs is neither a Democrat nor a Republican, but is instead a Socialist.

A conjunct is true when both of the conjoined propositions are true, but is false when either conjoined proposition is false. Thus "*p* & *q*" rules out three possibilities; namely, *p* true while *q* false, *p* false while *q* true, and *p* false while *q* false. The logical word "&" is the first so far encountered which eliminates more than one such possibility.

The *dilemma* is a complex argument which ancient logicians regarded as especially forceful, but which, from a modern point of view, seems no more important than any other. The peculiar "force" of a dilemma is, in fact, rhetorical rather than logical: a dilemma has the economy of expression of a limerick or triolet. In any event, the following argument is a dilemma:

(9.12) If I drive fast, I'll be in trouble; if I'm late for my appointment, I'll be in trouble.

I must either drive fast or be late for my appointment.

I'll be in trouble.

The structure of 9.12 is

(9.13) $(p \rightarrow q)$ & $(r \rightarrow q)$

$p \vee r$

q

A dilemma is called *constructive* when the second premise is the alternation of the antecedents of the conditionals conjoined in the first premise. It is *destructive* when the second premise is the alternation of the contradictories of the two consequents. Whereas 9.13 is constructive, the following dilemma is destructive:

(9.14) $(p \rightarrow q)$ & $(p \rightarrow r)$

$-q \vee -r$

$-p$

Dilemmas are also classified as "complex" or "simple," depending upon whether the conclusion is an alternation or not. Arguments

9.13 and 9.14 are both simple because neither has an alternative conclusion. The following dilemma is, on the other hand, complex:

(9.15) $(p \rightarrow q)$ & $(r \rightarrow s)$
$p \lor r$
——————————
$q \lor s$

The ancient logician felt trapped when faced by a dilemma, and sought general methods for disproving any such argument. One of these was called "taking the dilemma by the horns," and consisted of showing either of the conjoined conditionals to be false. Thus the conclusion of 9.12 is unwarranted if, in fact, I can drive fast without getting into trouble. Another method used to vitiate the force of a dilemma is to show that the alternatives of the second premise are not exhaustive; this is known as "escaping between the horns." I should escape between the horns of 9.12 were I to show that the place of my appointment is so near by that I needn't drive fast in order to be there on time. The reader should clearly realize, however, that these are considerations of fact only, and have no bearing upon the validity of 9.12. Like any other argument, 9.12 may be logically true even when some of its components are factually false.

The final sort of argument which we must consider in this section is one, the premises of which contain a phrase such as "if and only if." The force of this phrase, and others like it, is to express the equivalence of two propositions. The proposition "p if and only if q" means that p and q are equivalent; they are either both true or both false, and one may be substituted for the other in any context. Examples of equivalent propositions would be "Boggs died" and "Boggs's heart stopped beating permanently." What "Boggs died if and only if his heart stopped beating permanently" rules out is the possibility that the former might be true while the latter is false, or that the former might be false while the latter is true. If Boggs did not die, then it is likewise the case that his heart did not permanently stop beating.

Any proposition containing "if and only if" is known as a *biconditional*. This name suggests the fact that such a proposition is really the composite of a conditional and its converse. "Today is Monday if and only if tomorrow is Tuesday" means "If today is Monday, tomorrow is Tuesday; and if tomorrow is Tuesday, today is Monday." A biconditional thus expresses a *necessary* and *sufficient condition;* a necessary and sufficient condition for tomorrow's being Tuesday is that today is Monday.

To represent the kinship between conditionals and biconditionals, we shall employ the symbol "$\leftarrow\rightarrow$" for "if and only if" and other phrases having the same meaning. Given "$p \leftarrow\rightarrow q$" as a premise, it is possible to add other premises so as to argue in a number of ways. The reader should illustrate for himself each of the following valid structures, convincing himself of their general validity.

(9.16) $p \leftarrow\rightarrow q$
$\dfrac{p}{q}$

(9.17) $p \leftarrow\rightarrow q$
$\dfrac{q}{p}$

(9.18) $p \leftarrow\rightarrow q$
$\dfrac{-p}{-q}$

(9.19) $p \leftarrow\rightarrow q$
$\dfrac{-q}{-p}$

(9.20) $p \leftarrow\rightarrow q$
$q \leftarrow\rightarrow r$
$\overline{p \leftarrow\rightarrow r}$

(9.21) $p \leftarrow\rightarrow q$
$q \vee r$
$\overline{p \vee r}$

So many valid ways of arguing from a biconditional exist that it is difficult to imagine anyone committing a logical slip in this respect. Since it is useful to label fallacies only when people are apt to commit them, we shall give no name to those theoretically possible when a biconditional functions as the premise of an argument.

So much for the common modes of arguing when entire propositions are the variables. But these common modes do not by any means exhaust the possible structures; an infinite number of valid arguments may be constructed with the materials now at hand. This complexity is a cause for concern. So far, we have had to rely on common logical insight or intuition to see the validity of each argument in turn; what shall we do when an argument is so complex as to elude that intuition? We have as yet to produce a wholly general technique for dealing with propositional arguments. The following section will lay the groundwork for such a technique.

EXERCISES

A. The reader who did Part B of the exercises following Section 6 (page 36) was, in effect, asked to use common sense to decide whether each of seven conjunctive arguments was valid. Justify this common sense, or improve on it, by expressing each of these arguments in appropriate symbols and testing its validity according to the standards developed in the present section.

B. (a) Symbolize each of the following arguments, using the symbols suggested. (b) Identify the argument. (c) State whether it is valid.

1. Either Boggs is out or his telephone is out of order. But Boggs *is* out. Therefore, his telephone is not out of order. (B,T)
2. Either Boggs is out or his telephone is out of order. But Boggs is *not* out. Therefore, his telephone is out of order. (B,T)
3. It is not the case both that it is noon and that my watch is right. Since it is, in fact, noon, my watch must be wrong. (N,W)
4. It is not the case both that it is noon and that my watch is right. Since it is not, in fact, noon, my watch must be right. (N,W)

5. If I go over Niagara Falls in a barrel, I will surely die, but if I don't, I will die anyway.
   Either I'll go over Niagara Falls in a barrel or not

   I will die.   (N,D)

6. Diggs will be executed if and only if he was convicted of a capital crime.
   Diggs was not convicted of a capital crime.

   He will not be executed.   (D,C)

7. It is not the case both that Diggs was convicted of a capital crime and that he will not be executed.
   Diggs was not convicted of a capital crime.

   He will not be executed.   (D,C)

8. Boggs is either a carpenter or not a member of the union.
   He is a member of the union.

   He is a carpenter.   (C,M)

9. It is not the case both that Suggs is guillible and that Diggs is overanxious to please.
   Suggs is not gullible.

   Diggs is overanxious to please.   (S,D)

10. If Suggs testifies, he will face prosecution for conspiring to overthrow the government; if he does not testify, he will be cited for contempt of Congress.
    He must either testify or not testify.

    He will either face prosecution for conspiring to overthrow the government or be cited for contempt of Congress.   (T,P,C)

11. The ceremonies will take place either outdoors or indoors. For if the weather is fair, they will be held outdoors, while in case of rain, they will take place indoors. And there is no alternative to fair weather or rain.   (O,I,F,R)

12. It can't be true both that Diggs is an electrical engineer and that he is incapable of repairing a lamp cord. But he is not incapable of repairing a lamp cord. Therefore, he must be an electrical engineer.   (D,I)

13. Either there won't be a breeze or we'll go sailing.
    There won't be any breeze.

    We won't go sailing.   (B,S)

14. Either there won't be a breeze or we'll go sailing.
    There will be a breeze.

    We will go sailing.   (B,S)

15. If I am already rational, it is needless to study logic, and if not,

it is useless. But I am either already rational **or not.** Therefore, it is either needless or useless to study logic. (R,N,U)

16. It is not the case both that Meggs is a Democrat and his wife is a Republican.
Meggs is not a Democrat.
His wife is a Republican. (R,D)

17. It is not the case both that Meggs is not a Democrat and his wife is a Republican.
Meggs is not a Democrat.
His wife is not a Republican. (R,D)

18. If I am fated to fail the course, it is useless to study; if not, it is needless.
Either I am fated to fail the course or not.
It is either useless or needless to study. (F,N,U)

19. Either Boggs is a sophomore or my memory is incorrect.
Boggs is a sophomore.
My memory is correct. (B,C)

20. This triangle is equiangular if and only if it is equilateral.
This triangle is equiangular if and only if each angle is of 60 degrees.
This triangle is equilateral if and only if each angle is of 60 degrees. (EA,EL,60)

21. If I am to catch the bus, I must be at the depot in 15 minutes, and if I am to pass this test I must stay in class for 15 minutes. But either I can't get to the depot in 15 minutes or else I can't stay in class for 15 minutes. Hence I will either miss the bus or fail the test. (B,D,P,S)

22. The class does not meet today or the instructor is sick. The class does meet today. Therefore, the instructor is sick. (C,S)

23. The class does not meet today or the instructor is sick. The class does not meet today. Therefore, the instructor is not sick. (C,S)

24. Boggs could have won if and only if he had played flawlessly and his opponent had made a mistake.
Boggs lost.
He played flawlessly.
His opponent made no mistake. (B,F,M)
(*Hint:* Draw the conclusion from the biconditional argument involving the first two premises. Then see whether "-M" ac-

tually follows from that conclusion, together with the third premise.)

25. It is not the case both that it is midnight and the sun is shining. The sun is shining.
It is either noon or midnight.

It is noon.   (M,N,S)

(*Hint:* As in the case of No. 24, treat this as two distinct arguments, the conclusion of the first of which becomes a premise of the second.)

SUPPLEMENTARY READINGS

1. Herbert L. Searles, *Logic and Scientific Methods,* New York, The Ronald Press Company, 1948, Ch. 7.

2. Lionel Ruby, *Logic: An Introduction,* New York, J. B. Lippincott Company, 1950, Ch. 13.

3. Ralph M. Eaton, *General Logic,* New York, Charles Scribner's Sons, 1931, Pt. II, Ch. IV.

10

The Interrelations of Logical Words

We shall soon evolve a powerful mechanical technique for testing the validity of any propositional argument. The use of this technique will allow us to dispense with the need to intuit that a given argument is valid or invalid, and to deal with arguments so complex as to tax the intuition of anyone but a genius. A further virtue of the technique to be developed is that the theory on which it is based is simple. The preliminary aspects of the theory will be worked out in this section; their elucidation depends only on making explicit what has heretofore been implicit.

An important truth, hinted at throughout Sections 8 and 9, is that the logical words with which these sections deal bear a specific and definable relationship to each other. It was suggested in Section 9, for example, that the fallacy of alternation is tantamount to denying the antecedent or asserting the consequent of a conditional; if this is indeed true, then it must be possible to define "$\vee$" in terms of "$\rightarrow$," or vice versa. The meaning of "$p \leftarrow \rightarrow q$" was asserted to be that of "$p \rightarrow q$" conjoined with its converse; in this case, an outright definition of "$p \leftarrow \rightarrow q$" in terms of "$\rightarrow$" and "&" will be "$(p \rightarrow q) \ \& \ (q \rightarrow p)$." Again, the contradictory of "$p \rightarrow q$" is "p but not q" or (since "but" differs from "and" only rhetorically) "$p \ \& \ -q$." Because any proposition is equivalent to the denial of its own contradictory, "$p \rightarrow q$" is thus equivalent to

"-$(p \& -q)$." Let us now introduce some order into these observations.

We shall find that we can define each of the remaining logical words of Part Two in terms of "-" and "v." In the first place, "$p \& q$" means precisely, "-$(-p \vee -q)$." For instance, "It is raining & I am tired" means simply "It is not the case either that it is not raining or that I am not tired," that is, "-(-It is raining v -I am tired)." For the alternation "-p v -q" is the contradictory of "$p \& q$," since it permits precisely the possibilities that "$p \& q$" rules out (namely, that either or both p and q are false), and rules out the one possibility that "$p \& q$" permits (namely, that p and q are both true). But if "-p v -q," is the contradictory of "$p \& q$," then the denial of "-p v -q"—"-$(-p \vee -q)$"—is equivalent to "$p \& q$." The discovery of this relationship between "v" and "-," on the one hand, and "&" on the other is the first step in our systematizing.

The essential word "$\rightarrow$" can also be defined in terms of "v" and "-." For the exact meaning of "$p \rightarrow q$" is "-p v q." "If Boggs comes, Diggs will go" means neither more nor less than "Either Boggs will not come or Diggs will go"; since both rule out just the one possibility that Boggs will come and Diggs will not go. In ordinary speech, conditionals are often thrown into alternative form, whence they gain a new rhetorical flavor. The wife who says "Either you stop smoking cigars or I'll leave this house," means "If you don't stop smoking cigars, I'll leave this house"; and "It won't rain, or I'm a monkey's uncle" is equivalent to "If it rains, I'm a monkey's uncle."

We have already defined "$\leftarrow \rightarrow$" in terms of "$\rightarrow$"; "$p \leftarrow \rightarrow q$" is "$(p \rightarrow q) \& (q \rightarrow p)$." Since both "$\rightarrow$" and "&" are reducible to "v" and "-," we have theoretically satisfied the demand that "$\leftarrow \rightarrow$" be reducible. For practice, however, we shall carry out the actual reduction. Let us begin with the components "$p \rightarrow q$" and "$q \rightarrow p$." These reduce respectively to "-p v q" and "-q v p." Treating each of these as a simple proposition, we can now go to work on the symbol "&." Since "$p \& q$" reduces to "-$(-p \vee -q)$,"

(10.1) $(-p \vee q) \& (-q \vee p)$ reduces to -[-$(-p \vee q) \vee$ -$(-q \vee p)$]

It might be expected that some of the -'s would cancel each other out; it is surely true that --p is p in view of the Law of Double Negation, stated in Section 7. But no cancellation is possible in 10.1, because no proposition *as a whole* is negated twice. There is an analogy between negation in logic and the operation of the minus sign in arithmetic. The number -(-3) is simply 3; but special laws have to be introduced to allow us to handle such expressions as -(-3 + 4); no simple cancellation of minuses is permissible.

The reduction we have made in 10.1 is so complicated that in all probability no one of us can verify it through the unaided use of intuition. But we should not therefore look on 10.1 as a logical monstrosity. We should rather be encouraged by this palpable example of the way in which a symbolic technique can enhance our logical powers.

It is now possible to collect the definitions framed so far, under the *System of Alternation and Negation*. This system is as follows:

(10.2) Undefined Logical Words: - and v
  Definitions:
    (1) $p \& q$ means $-(-p \text{ v } -q)$
    (2) $p \rightarrow q$ means $-p \text{ v } q$
    (3) $p \longleftrightarrow q$ means $-(-(-p \text{ v } q) \text{ v } -(-q \text{ v } p))$

The System of Alternation and Negation is not, however, the only possible scheme for reducing all five of the logical words with which we are presently concerned to less than five. Another scheme is the *System of Conjunction and Negation,* which we shall simply state, leaving the reader to test for himself the definitions it proposes.

(10.3) Undefined Logical Words: - and &
  Definitions:
    (1) $p \text{ v } q$ means $-(-p \& -q)$
    (2) $p \rightarrow q$ means $-(p \& -q)$
    (3) $p \longleftrightarrow q$ means $(p \rightarrow q) \& (q \rightarrow p)$ or $-(p \& -q) \&$
      $-(q \& -p)$

Notice that definition (3) under 10.3 is more intelligible than the corresponding definition under 10.2. It stipulates that the possibilities that p might be true while q is false, or that q might be true while p is false, are both ruled out. But we have already pointed out that this is exactly what "$p \leftarrow \rightarrow q$" means.

Let us put some of our reductions to work. A logical law which has been acknowledged since ancient times is the *Law of the Excluded Middle, p* v *-p.* What this asserts is that any given proposition is either true or false; there is no middle ground. It is, for example, at the present moment, either raining or not raining. What happens when this law is expressed in terms of conjunction and negation?

By (1) of 10.3, "p v $-p$" means "$-(-p \ \& \ - -p)$." Here the last two -'s cancel out by the Law of Double Negation, since they both operate on the single proposition p. The result is "$-(-p \ \& \ p)$," and the classical name for this expression is the *Law of Contradiction.* The statement of this law is usually: "No proposition may be both true and false." Thus it cannot be both raining and not raining. Given any proposition and its contradictory, the Law of the Excluded Middle asserts that the two exhaust the alternatives, while the Law of Contradiction asserts that the two exclude each other. Thus p and $-p$ are exhaustive and exclusive alternatives; and to say they are exhaustive is to say they are exclusive, since one law reduces to the other.

Why is a fallacy of alternation the same as asserting the consequent or denying the antecedent of a conditional? The technique we have just begun to develop speedily supplies the answer even at this stage. There were two forms of the fallacy in question; namely

(10.4) p v q

p
___
$-q$

and

(10.5) $p \lor q$

$$\frac{q}{-p}$$

By (2) of system 10.2, the first premise in both 10.4 and 10.5 reduces to "$-p \rightarrow q$." Now p is the denial of $-p$; so if p is added as a premise, as it is in 10.4, the fallacy of concluding $-q$ is precisely that of denying the antecedent. And whoever argues to $-p$ after supplying q commits the fallacy of asserting the consequent.

To vindicate our definitions, we have relied partly on the demonstration that definiens and definiendum both rule out precisely the same possibilities of truth and falsehood. Thus "$p \lor q$" and "$-(-p$ & $-q)$" mean the same, because they both rule out the single case in which both p and q are false. We must now make explicit the reasoning underlying these rather casual "proofs" of equivalence. Let us begin by expressing in tabular form the possibilities of truth and falsehood which are open when "$p \lor q$" is given. Reading across,

(10.6)

When p is	and q is	then $p \lor q$ is
True	True	True
False	True	True
True	False	True
False	False	False

Thus the truth of "$p \lor q$" rules out only the possibility that p and q are both false. A more streamlined version of this "truth-table," embodying the form which we shall adopt for all such tables, is

(10.7)

p	$\lor$	q
T	T	T
F	T	T
T	T	F
F	F	F
1	2	1

Here the four possibilities of truth and falsehood are written under
the variables, and the effect of each of these possibilities on the
proposition "$p \vee q$" as a whole is written under the logical word
"$\vee$." It is convenient to speak of the truth or falsity of a proposition as its "truth-value." What we have just said may be re-
phrased: "The possible combinations of truth-value for p and q
are indicated under p and q respectively; and the resultant truth-
value of the expression as a whole is written under '$\vee$.'" The
number appearing at the foot of each column of truth-values indicates the order in which these values have been selected or com-
puted. In this example, 1 signifies the initial assignment of all
possible combinations of truth-values to p and q, and 2 represents
the respective resultant truth-values of "$p \vee q$" as a whole. In
more complex propositions, higher numbers will be needed; and
the highest of them will mark the column of truth-values for the
proposition as a whole, called the "main column." This numeri-
cal device has expository value only, and may be dropped in
practice.

When two distinct propositions, such as p and q, are ingredient
in a complex proposition, four possible combinations of truth-
value exist, as in 10.7. When three propositions are involved,
the truth-table must have eight rows, as we shall soon see. But
two rows suffice for the analysis by truth-table of a complex proposition in which one simple proposition is involved. The table,
below, for $-p$ illustrates this formula:

(10.8) - p

     F T

     T F

     2 1

Example 10.8 represents the fact that when p is true, $-p$ as a
whole is false, and when p is false, $-p$ is true. This is the simplest
truth-table we shall meet.

We now have truth-tables for both $p \vee q$ and $-p$; and we know
that $p \& q$ can be defined in terms of "$-$" and "$\vee$." These con-

siderations should enable us to discover the truth-table for *p & q*. Let us begin by writing out the definition and assigning to its propositional components their possible combinations of truth-values.

(10.9) *p & q* means -(- *p* v - *q*)

T	T
F	T
T	F
F	F
1	1

Working, as we should always, from the simplest of the component propositions to the most complex, we first fill in the columns under -*p* and -*q*.

(10.10) -(- *p* v - *q*)

FT	FT
TF	FT
FT	TF
TF	TF
21	21

The next step is to supply the appropriate truth-values for the proposition (-*p* v -*q*) as a whole. Since -*p* and -*q* are both false only in the first row, and since an alternation is false only when both of its components are false, an "F" will appear only in the first row.

(10.11) -(- *p* v - *q*)

FT	F	FT
TF	T	FT
FT	T	TF
TF	T	TF
21	3	21

Finally, we must supply the proper truth-values for the column under the outermost "-." Since the truth-table for -*p* is the reverse of that for *p*, the truth-values we must now add will be the reverse of those under the v.

(10.12)   - (- p v - q)
          T FT F FT
          F TF T FT
          F FT T TF
          F TF T TF
          4 21 3 21

Now the main column of 10.12 shows what truth-values must be written under the & of p & q when p and q assume the respective truth-values they have in 10.12.   Therefore, the truth-table for p & q is as follows:

(10.13) p & q
          T   T   T
          F   F   T
          T   F   F
          F   F   F
          1   2   1

Nothing could jibe better with our expectations; nothing could serve better to verify the definition of "&" rendered in 10.12.   For what 10.13 tells us is that p & q can be true only when p and q are both true.   And this is precisely what p & q means.

We shall derive only a few other truth-tables here; the student should work out tables for the words defined in 10.3, taking 10.8 and 10.13 as the tables for the undefined words.   But something special should be remarked about the truth-table for →.   If "p → q" means "-p v q," and the truth table for the latter is

(10.14) - p v q
          F T T T
          T F T T
          F T F F
          T F T F
          2 1 3 1

then the truth-table for p → q is

(10.15) $p \rightarrow q$

```
T T T
F T T
T F F
F T F
1 2 1
```

Now 10.15 does accurately represent the fact that a true conditional cannot have its antecedent true and its consequent false; this shows up in the third row.   But we may suspect that 10.15 commits us to more than we are willing to assert.   In particular, it commits us to the view that *any conditional is true when its antecedent is false or its consequent is true*.   For example, if 10.15 is correct, the following propositions will be true:

(10.16) Lead floats on water $\rightarrow$ water is a fluid.
(10.17) Lead floats on water $\rightarrow$ water is a solid.

Note, however, that neither 10.16 nor 10.17 is a valid argument, since the truth of both depends upon the factual falsity of their antecedents.   The value of asserting that 10.16 and 10.17 are true is only to exhibit the effect of this truth-value upon the more complex structures in which they occur, such as valid arguments which might contain them.   In any event, ordinary English is uncertain about the truth or falsity of conditionals whose antecedents are false.   "If I jump out of this window, I shall be killed" is certainly true even though its antecedent is now false; and people often use such expressions as "If the Dodgers win, I'll eat my hat," without the slightest intent of actually fulfilling the consequent. Other cases, however, might be mentioned in which everyday usage takes a conditional with a false antecedent to be false.   In such situations, the logician can do no better than to take up one option and adhere consistently to it.   The option which the logician chooses is that a conditional is true whenever its antecedent is false or its consequent is true.

Since "$p \longleftrightarrow q$" means "$(p \rightarrow q)$ & $(q \rightarrow p)$," its truth-table is the following:

(10.18) $(p \rightarrow q)$ & $(q \rightarrow p)$

```
T T T   T   T T T
F T T   F   T F F
T F F   F   F T T
F T F   T   F T F
1 2 1   3   1 2 1
```

Notice that when a simple proposition, such as p or q above, occurs more than once within a complex proposition whose truth-table is to be derived, it must be given the same set of truth-values whenever it occurs. If p is true, as it is in the first and third rows of the first column of 10.18, then it must be true in the same rows under any other of its occurrences in 10.18; specifically, it is true in the first and third rows of the last column. Similar considerations hold for the truth-values of q. These remarks follow from the Law of Contradiction; a proposition cannot be both true and false at the same time.

The column under the "&" in 10.18 is exactly as we should have expected, since it means that "$p \leftarrow \rightarrow q$" is true when its components agree in truth-value, and false when they do not. That is, the two possibilities ruled out by the truth of "$p \leftarrow \rightarrow q$" are that p might be true while q is false, or that q might be true while p is false. Having grasped the significance of 10.18, let us turn to a truth-table which we can now construct, namely, that for -p $\leftarrow \rightarrow q$.

(10.19)   -p $\leftarrow \rightarrow$ q

```
F T   F   T
T F   T   T
F T   T   F
T F   F   F
2 1   3   1
```

This table represents a complex proposition in which p and q are ingredients, and which is false when, and only when, p and q are both true or both false. In Section 9 we noted the need to express the notion of the *exclusive "or"*; this table expresses it precisely. When "*p* or *q*, but not both" is true, then the simultaneous truth of both *p* and *q* is ruled out, as is their simultaneous falsehood. The previous example, "Either Boggs is male or Boggs is female," expresses the notion in words. If we so desired, we might adopt a special symbol for the exclusive "or," defining it as "-*p* ← → *q*." No purpose, however, is served by the multiplication of symbols beyond the dictates of necessity. We need only point out that when *p* and *q* are joined by an exclusive "or," the complex proposition which they form is the *contradictory* of "*p* ← → *q*."

We stand now on the verge of a completely general technique for testing the validity of propositional arguments. Only one other simple idea, that of a *tautology,* is necessary to insure success. That notion will be expounded in Section 11. Meanwhile, we should not let an important fact, brought out in the present section, go unnoticed: whenever a complex proposition consists of two or more simple propositions joined by a logical word, the truth-value of the whole depends entirely upon the truth-values of its components. Thus we may calculate the truth-value of "*p* v *q*" if we know, for example, that *p* is true and *q* is false. Similarly, if *p* and *q* are both false, it follows that "-*p* & -*q*" is true. Now any proposition, the truth-value of which is computable from the truth-values of its components, is called a *truth-function.*

The procedure for calculating or computing the truth-value of a truth-function is known as the *Propositional Calculus.* In its ordinary acceptation, "calculus" is a frightening word to many people. But correct English usage does not restrict the application of this word to discourse about integrals and differentials; a calculus is any method of calculating, including fourth-grade arithmetic and the "hedonistic calculus" of pleasures and pains which the moralist Jeremy Bentham advocated. "Calculus" is the Latin word for "pebble," a fact which suggests the simplicity of the Roman methods of calculating. We shall turn now to an elaboration of the Propositional Calculus.

EXERCISES

A. Express each of the following propositions in terms of conjunction and denial.   Use the symbols C,M.

1. It is cold or the moon is shining.
2. If it is cold, the moon is shining.
3. It is cold if, and only if, the moon is shining.
4. If it is cold, the moon is not shining.
5. If the moon is not shining, it is not cold.
6. It is cold or the moon is not shining.
7. It is not the case either that it is not cold or that the moon is not shining.
8. It is not the case that if it is cold, then the moon is shining.
9. It is not cold if, and only if, the moon is shining.
10. It is cold or the moon is shining, but not both.

B. Express each of the following propositions in terms of alternation and denial.   Use symbols W,J.

1. Today is Wednesday and it is June 21st.
2. If today is Wednesday, it is June 21st.
3. If today is Wednesday, it is not June 21st.
4. If today is not Wednesday, it is June 21st.
5. If today is June 21st, it is Wednesday.
6. It is not both Wednesday and June 21st.
7. It is not both Wednesday and not June 21st.
8. It is not both not Wednesday and not June 21st.
9. It is not the case that if it is Wednesday, then it is June 21st.
10. It is not the case that if it is June 21st, then it is Wednesday.

C. Construct the System of Implication and Negation.   That is, define each of the symbols "v," "&," and "← →" in terms of "→" and "-."

D. Using the principle that, when two complex propositions have the same main column of truth-values in their respective truth-tables, then they must have the same meaning, determine which of the following propositions have the same meaning as "$p \rightarrow -q$":

1. $p \vee q$
2. $-p \vee q$

3. $p \lor -q$
4. $-p \lor -q$
5. $p \,\&\, q$
6. $-p \,\&\, q$
7. $-(p \,\&\, q)$
8. $p \longleftrightarrow -q$
9. $q \to -p$
10. $-q \to p$
11. $(-p \lor -q) \,\&\, (p \lor -p)$
12. $(-p \lor -q) \,\&\, (q \to -p)$
13. $(-p \lor -q) \lor (q \to -p)$
14. $(-p \lor -q) \lor (p \,\&\, -p)$
15. $(-p \lor -q) \lor (p \lor -p)$
16. $(-p \lor -q) \,\&\, (p \,\&\, -p)$
17. $(p \lor q) \,\&\, -(p \,\&\, q)$
18. $p \to (q \to -q)$
19. $(p \to p) \to (q \to -q)$
20. $p \to [(p \to q) \to -q]$

SUPPLEMENTARY READINGS

1. Irving M. Copi, *Introduction to Logic,* New York, The Macmillan Company, 1953, Ch. 8.

2. W. H. Werkmeister, *An Introduction to Critical Thinking,* Lincoln, Nebraska, Johnsen Publishing Company, 1948, Pt. III, Ch. XIII.

3. Alice Ambrose and Morris Lazerowitz, *Fundamentals of Symbolic Logic,* New York, Rinehart & Company, Inc., 1948, Ch. III.

11

The Tautology

The Law of the Excluded Middle was stated in Section 10, and the reduction of this law to conjunction and denial sufficed to reveal it as merely a version of the Law of Contradiction. (Another version is, of course, "$p \rightarrow p$," since this reduces to "$-(p \& -p)$.") We did not, however, write down the *truth-table* for this law in any of its versions. Let us do so now.

(11.1) $p \quad v \quad -p$
       T T FT
       F T TF
       1 3 21

(11.2) $- (p \& -p)$
       T T F FT
       T F F TF
       4 1 3 21

(11.3) $p \quad \rightarrow \quad p$
       T T T
       F T F
       1 2 1

Each of these versions, then, receives the same column of truth-values, namely, TT. This is the first time such an assignment has been possible; heretofore, every truth-function has had to be assigned at least one "F" in its main column. What does a solid column of T's mean? In the correct reply to this question resides the germ of the idea to be developed throughout this section.

The assignment of "T" to the main column of each of 11.1, 11.2, and 11.3, means that any of these versions of the Law of Contradiction is true both when *p* is true and when *p* is false. This is to say, the truth of the law is independent of the truth or falsehood of *p*. But since the truth or falsehood of *p* may well depend in turn on a fact, circumstance, situation, or state of affairs, it follows that the *truth of the Law of Contradiction is independent of any fact, circumstance, situation, or state of affairs.* To put the matter more simply, the law is a logical truth—and *this* is the significance of the solid column of T's.

Let us take a more complicated example, say, "(*p* & *q*) → (*p* v *q*)." For this example, the following truth-table is derivable:

(11.4) (*p* & *q*) → (*p* v *q*)

T	T	T	T	T	T	T
F	F	T	T	F	T	T
T	F	F	T	T	T	F
F	F	F	T	F	F	F
1	2	1	3	1	2	1

Again, the main column of truth-values for 11.4 as a whole consists entirely of T's. Thus the truth of 11.4 is independent of any set of truth-values which might be assigned to either *p* or *q* by virtue of facts. Therefore 11.4 is a logical truth.

The last logical truth of this sort that we now shall examine affords practice with an eight-row truth-table. It is "[(*p* v *q*) & *r*] ← → [(*p* & *r*) v (*q* & *r*)]," and is known as the *Principle of Distributivity,* since it sanctions the distribution of any proposition conjoined with an alternation across that alternation. The required table is as follows:

(11.5) $[(p \lor q) \ \& \ r] \longleftrightarrow [(p \ \& \ r) \lor (q \ \& \ r)]$

T	T	T	T	T	T	T	T	T	T	T	T
F	T	T	T	T	T	F	F	T	T	T	T
T	T	F	T	T	T	T	T	T	T	F	F
F	F	F	F	T	T	F	F	T	F	F	F
T	T	T	F	F	T	T	F	F	F	T	F
F	T	T	F	F	T	F	F	F	F	T	F
T	T	F	F	F	T	T	F	F	F	F	F
F	F	F	F	F	T	F	F	F	F	F	F
1	2	1	3	1	4	1	2	1	3	1	2	1

Because the main column under the "&" on the left side is the same as the main column under the "∨" on the right, we cannot but conclude that the biconditional joining left to right must receive a T in each of its rows. Thus 11.5 is logically true. In passing, notice how truth-values were successively assigned to each of three different variables so as to exhaust the possible combinations.

This should be a sufficient introduction to the notion of a tautology. *A tautology is any truth-function whose truth-value is always "T."* Each of the tables 11.1 through 11.5 represents a tautology. All tautologies are logically true propositions; but not every logically true proposition is a tautology. In Part Three, in fact, we shall be concentrating on logical truths which are *not* tautologies.

Now we have reached the point at which the developments of the present part begin to bear fruit. We want a general technique for testing the validity of any propositional argument. An argument is valid only when it is logically true. But a propositional argument is always a truth-function; the only logical words it contains are those for which a truth-table might be constructed. A logically true truth-function is a tautology. Therefore, *every valid propositional argument is a tautology.*

We have hitherto written arguments vertically, separating premises from conclusion by means of a horizontal line. In order to test them by means of truth-tables, we shall have to express these arguments horizontally. But this only involves remembering that the horizontal line is a symbol for implication; specifically, the implication holding between premises and conclusion. We can also perceive now that when an argument has more than one premise, these premises are joined by an implicit or explicit "&," as in "Boggs is a Communist → Boggs advocates revolution, *and* Boggs is a Communist." Thus any argument can be written out horizontally, if the appropriate "&"s are supplied, and the horizontal line is replaced by "→." Since the validity of an argument hinges on the logical truth of the implication, it is under the "→" connecting the conjunction of the premises with the conclusion that we must look for the solid column of T's guaranteeing validity.

Let us rephrase some earlier structures, and test their validity. *Modus ponens* was

$$p \to q$$
$$\underline{p}$$
$$q$$

It now becomes

$$[(p \to q) \ \& \ p] \to q$$

the truth-table for which reads

(11.6)

[(p	→	q)	&	p]	→	q
T	T	T	T	T	T	T
F	T	T	F	F	T	T
T	F	F	F	T	T	F
F	T	F	F	F	T	F
1	2	1	3	1	4	1

The absence of any F from the column of truth-values under the main "→" to the right thus warrants the assertion that *modus ponens* is valid. A similar table can be constructed to evince the validity of *modus tollens*. The fallaciousness of denying the antecedent, on the other hand, is made clear by the following truth-table:

(11.7) $[(p \rightarrow q)$ & $- p] \rightarrow - q$

T	T	T	F	FT	T	FT
F	T	T	T	TF	F	FT
T	F	F	F	FT	T	TF
F	T	F	F	TF	T	TF
1	2	1	3	21	4	21

The appearance of F in the second row under the main "$\rightarrow$" shows that 11.7 fails whenever p happens to be false and q true. But since the converse of "$p \rightarrow q$" is false under these circumstances, this is no more than to say that the danger of denying the antecedent of a conditional is that its converse might well be false. In particular, one may not argue

> Boggs votes $\rightarrow$ Boggs is over twenty-one
>
> -Boggs votes
> _____
>
> -Boggs is over twenty-one,

because the antecedent of the first premise might well be false while the consequent is true; in other words, because the converse of the first premise is not true.

The appearance of one F or more in the main column of the truth-table for any argument always indicates that the argument in question is invalid. For, in such a case, the implication between premises and conclusion will fail whenever the variables assume appropriate truth-values. Factual considerations may render it impossible for the variables ever to assume the telltale truth-values which would falsify the argument. It is conceivable, for example, that all people over twenty-one *do* vote, so that the situation in which it is false that Boggs votes but true that he is over twenty-one might never, in fact, be possible. But then the truth of the argument will hinge on considerations which are factual rather than logical. And no argument is valid unless it is logically true.

One final truth-table should suffice for expository purposes. This is the table which proves the validity of the chain argument. Since three variables occur in

$$p \rightarrow q$$
$$q \rightarrow r$$
$$\overline{p \rightarrow r}$$

this table will require eight rows, as follows:

(11.8) $[(p \rightarrow q) \text{ \& } (q \rightarrow r)] \rightarrow (p \rightarrow r)$

T	T		T	T	T	T T	T		T T
F	T		T	T	T	F	T T		
T	F		F	T	T	T	T T		
F	F		F	T	T	F	T T		
T T T	F	T F F	T	T	F F				
F	T		T	F	T	F	T F		
T F F	F	F T F	T	T	F F				
F	F		F	F	T	F	T F		
1	2 1	3	1	2 1		4	1	2 1	

The incompleteness of 11.8 is to suggest a shortcut for working out the truth-tables of complex conditional propositions. Whenever the consequent of a conditional is true we know that the conditional as a whole is true regardless of the truth-value of its antecedent; therefore there is no need to compute this truth-value in such a case. It is only when the consequent is false that we must worry about the truth-value of the antecedent. Thus we may appreciably curtail our task by computing first the column of truth-values for the consequent; we need then to deal with the antecedent only in those rows where the consequent is false.

The principle just applied can, in fact, be used to reduce our work still further. Whenever a truth-function has the over-all form of a conditional proposition, the only truth-values which need be assigned to the consequent are those which render it false. And having made such an assignment, all we need then do is to inquire whether the antecedent can be true. For 11.8, the only such assignment possible is

(11.9) $(p \rightarrow r)$

T F F

Giving these values to p and r respectively, as they occur in the antecedent, we obtain for the latter,

(11.10) $[(p \to q)$ & $(q \to r)]$
                T   F

But whatever truth-value we now assign to q, 11.10 will necessarily be false.   For if q is true, then "$(q \to r)$" is false, and so, likewise, is the conjunct of which the latter is a member.   And if q is false, so is "$(p \to q)$," and thus the antecedent as a whole.   The antecedent cannot, therefore, be false when its consequent is false; this discovery is sufficient to establish that 11.8 is a tautology.

The denial of a tautology is called a *contradiction;* the main column under a contradiction consists wholly of F's.   Any contradiction is logically false, because its falsity is independent of the factual truth or falsity of its components.   The proposition "p & $-p$" exemplifies the idea of a contradiction.   So does "$-(p \to p)$."

All contradictions are equivalent to each other, and all tautologies are mutually equivalent.   For suppose p and q are both contradictions.   Then each has under it a solid column of F's.   In this case "$p \longleftrightarrow q$," which expresses the equivalence of p and q, will be a tautology.   Similarly, tautologies themselves are equivalent, agreeing as they do in truth-value.

Not only are all tautologies equivalent, but in general all logically true propositions are equivalent.   For they are true under all circumstances.   Similarly, any logical falsehood always has the truth-value F.   It follows that there will be no ambiguity if we decide to employ a single symbol to represent any tautologous proposition, or logical truth whatsoever, and another symbol to represent any contradiction, or logical falsehood.   We therefore propose the letter t to represent the former, and the letter f to stand for the latter.

Let us consider the logical relations among tautologies, contradictions, and other propositions.   What happens, for instance, when a tautology is conjoined with another proposition?   We have only to work out the truth-table for this conjunction.

(11.11) *t* & *p*

T T T
T F F
1 2 1

This table means that the conjunction of a tautology with any given proposition leaves the logical significance of that proposition wholly unaltered.   "It is either raining or not raining, and I am going to town" means precisely, "I am going to town," because, as 11.11 informs us, the former is true when the latter is true and false when it is false.   So "*t* & *p*" is equivalent to *p*.

The conjunction of a contradiction with a given proposition is, on the other hand, always a contradiction, thus

(11.12) *f* & *p*

F F T
F F F
1 2 1

It follows that "It is both raining and not raining, and I am going to town" would be false in any conceivable world.

For analogous reasons, "*t* v *p*" is equivalent with *t*, and "*f* v *p*" means precisely *p*.   The proposition "*t* ← → *p*" means *p*, and "*f* ← → *p*" means -*p*.   Consider now the various possible combinations involving implication.   These are

(11.13) *f* → *p*

F T T
F T F
1 2 1

(11.14) *p* → *t*

T T T
F T T
1 2 1

(11.15) *p* → *f*

T F F
F T F
1 2 1

(11.16) $t \rightarrow p$

    T T T

    T F F

    1 2 1

These four tables, respectively, indicate that a contradiction implies any proposition whatsoever; that a tautology is implied by any proposition one might select; that "$p \rightarrow f$" is equivalent to -p; and that "$t \rightarrow p$" is equivalent to p.   The first table gives in compact form an account of the relationship between logic and communication.   For it asserts that anything follows from a contradiction. Thus 11.13 incisively and emphatically answers the query, "Why should one be logical?"   One should be logical because, if he is not, every thinkable proposition, whether true or false, is implied by his assertions.   One's words will no longer permit the distinction between true and false in what follows from them.   They will, therefore, no longer convey information—at which point one has ceased to communicate with other people.

A lie is a deliberate contradiction.   Because the chaotic consequences of the lie may not be perceived immediately, the liar can often achieve expedient results through his lie.   But his destiny is to cut himself completely off from a society for which his utterances have become meaningless, and to which he can therefore no longer turn for succor.   The liar threatens society as well as himself, for he undermines the very condition which makes communication possible—that it be consistent.

A less vivid but no less important lesson is to be learned from 11.16, above.   This truth-table informs us that "$t \rightarrow p$" holds only where p is true.   If the proposition "$t \rightarrow p$" is to be a logical truth, then p must itself be a logical truth.   This bears out a remark made in Section 5 (page 28): a logical truth implies nothing interesting, only other logical truths.   It was for this reason that we concluded that no fact about the world could be deduced from any "fundamental" set of logically true assumptions.

Tables 11.11 and 11.12, as well as the remarks immediately following them, suggest a certain analogy between the propositional calculus on the one hand and algebra on the other. The expression "*t* & *p*," for instance, is like the expression "1 times *a*," in that the former reduces to *p* and the latter to *a*. Similarly, the equivalence of "*f* & *p*" with *f* is isomorphic with the equation "0 times *a* equals 0." The possibility that *f* has the same function as 0 is further substantiated by the similarity between "*f* v *p*" and "0 plus *a*"; the former reduces to *p*, and the latter to *a*. An anomaly, however, exists in the case of "*t* v *p*" and "1 plus *a*"; the former is equivalent with *t*, while the latter is not generally identical with 1. But this very anomaly has been exploited to give rise to a powerful new kind of algebra in which "1 plus *a*" does equal 1. Among the consequences of this assumption are the following:

> *a* times *a* equals *a*
> *a* plus *a* equals *a*
> Minus (*a* times *b*) equals minus *a* plus minus *b*.

This last equation recognizes the similarity between the logical "-" and the algebraic "minus." In addition, "← →" is like "equals" and "→" is like "less than." Just as "*f* → *p*" is true, so is "0 is less than any number, *a*."

This new kind of algebra is called "Boolean algebra," after its inventor, George Boole, whose book, *An Investigation of the Laws of Thought* (1854), set the stage for modern logic and the consequent overthrow of the ancient tradition in logic. Boole began with the algebra just mentioned; the bearing of this algebra on the logic of propositions was not noticed until somewhat later.

The significance of Boolean algebra is that it permits us to deal expeditiously with classes of things regardless of the sizes of these classes. Among the problems which Boole was able to solve, for instance, was the following:

> Given that "Wealth consists of things transferable, limited in supply, and either productive of pleasure or preventive of pain," to determine what things are limited in supply, as dependent upon their relation to wealth, transferableness, and tendency to produce pleasure, omitting all reference to the prevention of pain.

For Boole's answer, see *The Laws of Thought,* page 108. Now-adays Boolean algebra is used to solve similar problems which arise in fields as diverse as life insurance and electrical engineering.

EXERCISES

A. Use truth-tables to determine the validity or invalidity of each of the following structures.

1. *Modus tollens.*
2. Asserting the consequent.
3. An invalid chain argument.
4. *Reductio ad absurdum.*
5. A valid form of alternative argument.
6. An invalid form of alternative argument.
7. A valid form of conjunctive argument.
8. An invalid form of conjunctive argument.
9. Simple constructive dilemma.
10. Complex destructive dilemma.

B. Use the abbreviated truth-table method discussed toward the end of this section to determine whether each of the following arguments is valid or invalid. In other words, (a) assign truth values to the propositions comprising the conclusion in such a way that the conclusion as a whole is false; then (b) see whether, under these circumstances, the premises can all be true. If they can, the argument is invalid; otherwise, it is valid. Use the symbols suggested.

1. If it does not rain, and I do not lose my way, I shall visit you on Saturday. I shall not lose my way. Therefore, either it will rain or I shall visit you on Saturday. (R,L,V)
2. The engine will start only if the key is turned and the starter-button is pressed. I have turned the key. Therefore, if I press the starter-button the engine will start. (E,K,S)
3. Sugg's report either is not significant or it is different from the account Meggs gave. But it cannot be both different from the account Meggs gave and at the same time true. Therefore if Sugg's report is untrue, it is not significant. (S,D,T)
4. If business has fallen off, then, if sales-prospects are favorable,

Meggs is out of town. Since Meggs is in town, therefore either business has not fallen off or sales-prospects are unfavorable. (B,S,M)

5. If the missing woman either lost her way and fell into quicksand or suffered amnesia and went to Boston, it follows that if she did not go to Boston, then if she lost her way, she fell into quicksand. (L,Q,A,B)

6. If this substance is soluble, then if it is placed in water it will dissolve. But it does not dissolve. Therefore it is either not soluble or not placed in water. (S,W,D)

7. If this substance is soluble, then if it is placed in water it will dissolve. But it is not placed in water. Therefore it is either not soluble or it does not dissolve. (S,W,D)

8. Either Suggs does not intend to come, or he missed his train. If he missed his train, he will send a wire. Therefore, if he does not intend to come, he will not send a wire. (I,M,W)

9. Diggs will win if and only if he plays flawlessly and his opponent makes a mistake. But his opponent will make no mistake. Therefore, Diggs cannot win. (W,F,M)

10. Today is Monday, if it is December 11th and this year is 1950. But since today is not Monday, either it is not December 11th or this year is not 1950. (M,D,Y)

C. Use truth-tables to decide whether each of the following statements is true or false.

1. The alternation of a given proposition with itself means the same as that proposition.

2. The conjunction of a given proposition with itself is a tautology.

3. When a certain proposition implies its own contradictory, the result is a contradiction.

4. If p implies q, then p implies "q or r."

5. Given any two propositions p and q, either p implies q or q implies p.

6. Given any two propositions p and q, one or the other must be true.

7. Given any two propositions p and q, where "$q \longleftrightarrow -p$," one or the other must be true.

8. Any contradiction implies any tautology.

9. If a certain proposition q is implied both by another proposition p and by the denial of p, then q is true.

10. "P or q, possibly both" implies "p or q, but not both."

SUPPLEMENTARY READINGS

1. John Cooley, *A Primer of Formal Logic,* New York, The Macmillan Company, 1942, Ch. Two.

2. Alice Ambrose and Morris Lazerowitz, *Fundamentals of Symbolic Logic,* New York, Rinehart & Company, Inc., 1948, Ch. VI.

3. W. H. Werkmeister, *An Introduction to Critical Thinking,* Lincoln, Nebraska, Johnsen Publishing Company, 1948, Pt. III, Ch. XIII.

On Boolean Algebra

4. Louis Couturat, *The Algebra of Logic,* translated by Lydia G. Robinson, Chicago, The Open Court Publishing Co., 1914.

PART THREE

The Logic of Classes

12

The Analysis of Propositions

The validity of any argument in which all the unessential words are propositions as a whole may be tested by the methods developed in Part Two. These methods are both general and economical; they apply to all propositional arguments, and their application is simple and straightforward. But we must now acknowledge an indefinitely large group of arguments to which truth-table techniques do not apply. As arguments go, many of them are far from complicated; no truth-table, for example, can be constructed to test the validity of the exceedingly simple argument

(12.1) Some Representatives are women.

Some women are Representatives.

If the structure of 12.1 could be symbolized in terms of logical words and propositional variables alone, we should have to represent this structure by

(12.2) p

q

for "Some Representatives are women" and "Some women are Representatives" express different propositions. But 12.2 is clearly invalid; "$p \to q$" is not a tautology. It might be objected here that we should have used the *same* variable for "Some Representatives are women" and "Some women are Representatives," since these two propositions are equivalent. But this begs the question: "*Are* these two propositions equivalent?" The question is not answered by assuming that they are.

The equivalence of the two propositions in question can be established only if 12.1 is seen to exhibit a structure of essential and inessential words which warrants its assertion independently of any fact. The peculiar structure which 12.1 does exhibit is

(12.3) Some ———— are *****.
        ─────────────────────────
        Some ***** are ————.

Now the blanks, or variables, of 12.3 are not replaceable by propositions; rather nouns must be supplied. But truth-tables apply only to structures all of whose variables are replaceable by propositions. Thus the general equivalence of the premise and conclusion of 12.3 cannot be established by means of any truth-table.

Again, the so-called "categorical syllogism" falls outside the scope of the tautology. A definition of this sort of argument will be provided in Section 14 (page 132); an example of the categorical syllogism is the following:

(12.4) All whales are mammals.
        All mammals are vertebrates.
        ─────────────────────────
        All whales are vertebrates.

The attempt to cast this in the form of a propositional argument results in

(12.5) p
        q
        ───
        r

which is not valid. Instead, the validity of 12.4 depends on its inner structure of logical words and inessential nouns, namely,

(12.6) All ———— are *****.
        All ***** are /////.
        ─────────────────────────
        All ———— are /////.

Because the variables stand for nouns, the method of truth-tables would once more fail to be effective. Another reason for this failure is the consideration that logical words other than "-," "v," "&," "→," and so on, occur in 12.6. These other words, such as "all" and "are," have yet to be defined, either in terms of truth-tables or otherwise.

Structures 12.3 and 12.6 represent the arguments to which we shall now turn. The validity of these arguments depends not only upon the way in which propositions as a whole are related, but also upon the inner structures of the related propositions. The validity of 12.6, for instance, hinges on the arrangement of blanks *within* the propositions constituting its premises and conclusion. These blanks are variables for nouns or adjectives.

It is convenient to refer to what is denoted by a noun or an adjective as a *class*. A class may be construed as either a group of objects possessing some property in common, or that property itself. Thus, the noun "whales" in "All whales are mammals" denotes the collection of things having a certain complex property which involves, among other things, the characteristics of aquatic habitat and lung-respiration. In "All whales are gray," "gray" denotes either a chromatic property or the collection of all the things in the world having this property. No purpose of this book will be defeated if we consider "All whales are gray" and "All whales are gray things" to have exactly the same meaning.

By a *term* we mean any word denoting a class. In other words, a term is a noun or adjective. And 12.3 and 12.6 differ from the arguments analyzed in Part Two primarily in that their inessential words are terms rather than entire propositions.

Any argument containing inessential terms will be said to belong to the *Logic of Classes*. This branch of logic investigates the bearing of variables for classes (*class-variables* or *term-variables*) on the validity of arguments. And it scrutinizes the meanings of logical words, such as "All," "some," "is," and "are," which do not occur in propositional arguments. But it does not disregard the words which join propositions as a whole, since these, too, are essential to arguments involving class-variables. For these arguments are still arguments, so that implication is still essential between premises and conclusion, and the premises are still joined by conjunction. And any of the other words analyzed in Part Two could properly occur in an argument in which class-variables also occurred. Thus there is an important sense in which the logic of classes *includes* the logic of propositions. The former is an extension of the latter, enriched by new logical words, and incapable of being tested by truth-tables.

Since we are now essentially concerned with classes, we ought to consider how the terms denoting them figure within propositions. In thus analyzing propositions we shall, of course, be abandoning our previous treatment of the simple proposition as the ultimate unit unessential to a valid argument. Historically, however, the proposition was split into simpler components long before it was recognized as capable of entering atomically into logical truth. The traditional analysis of the proposition is that first given by Aristotle (384-322 B.C.). In addition, there is a modern treatment of the inner structure of propositions, which we shall sketch out after discussing in some detail the Aristotelian conception and its consequences.

According to the traditional Aristotelian point of view, each simple proposition involves just two terms, a *subject* and a *predicate*. The *subject* denotes the class *about which* the proposition makes an assertion or denial, and the predicate denotes the class *asserted* or *denied* of the subject. "Whales are gray" thus asserts the predicate *gray* of the subject *whales*. "A liquid is not a gas" denies the predicate *gas* of the subject *liquid*. And in "Boggs is a Communist," *Boggs* is the subject, and *Communist* the predicate.

There are certain kinds of propositions, the analysis of which on this scheme requires ingenuity. "It is raining" must be paraphrased as "Rain is now falling," because otherwise it lacks a subject. "Venus is between Earth and Mercury" would seem to involve three terms instead of two only; in such a case, "between Earth and Mercury" must be treated as a single predicate. There is no general formula for ascertaining the subject and the predicate of a proposition, but it is obvious that no proposition could be so anomalous as altogether to resist analysis of this sort. If one views propositions as fundamentally constituted of subject and predicate, then one will not scruple to treat the stubborn cases somewhat arbitrarily, since only the possibility of such treatment will prove that these cases should be regarded as propositions at all. The table which follows gives some further samples of propositions analyzed into subject and predicate. In general, one attempts to render every verb, together with its object, as a predicate nominative, which will then appear after the copulative verb "is" or "are." The grammatical subject of the sentence is similarly paraphrased as a suitable subject for the copulative verb.

Proposition	*Paraphrase* (subject underlined once, predicate twice)
1. Meggs smokes	Meggs is a smoker
2. Meggs smokes Fumettes	Meggs is a smoker of Fumettes
3. All who smoke Fumettes cough	All smokers of Fumettes are coughers
4. Whenever I smoke a Fumette, I cough	All times when I smoke a Fumette are times when I cough
5. Meggs gives a Fumette to Boggs	Meggs is a person who gives a Fumette to Boggs

There are several ways in which the predicate of a proposition might be related to the subject. As we have indicated, for example, the predicate might be *affirmed* or *denied* of the subject. Adopting the symbols S for Subject and P for Predicate, we may express these two relationships in general by saying that "S is P" is an *affirmative* proposition, while "S is not P" is *negative*.

A proposition might concern all of its subject, or just a part of it; "All *S* is *P*" is a *universal* proposition, whereas "Some *S* is *P*" is *particular*. In the examples used in this section "All whales are mammals" is universal, and "Some Representatives are women" is particular. But how are we to regard "Boggs is a Communist"? The question "Are we dealing with all of Boggs or only part of him?" seems odd. In practice, however, we shall treat this, and all other propositions whose subjects are single entities or individuals, as universal.

Both universal and particular propositions may be either affirmative or negative. Thus four sorts of propositions are possible:

	Universal	*Particular*
Affirmative	All *S* is *P*	Some *S* is *P*
Negative	No *S* is *P*	Some *S* is not *P*

We shall find it convenient to abbreviate further these standard forms which propositions may take. Thus

"All *S* is *P*" is abbreviated *A*
"Some *S* is *P*" is abbreviated *I*
"Some *S* is not *P*" is abbreviated *O*
"No *S* is *P*" is abbreviated *E*

These abbreviations are of considerable antiquity. They are derived from the first two vowels of the Latin verbs *affirmo* ("I affirm") and *nego* ("I deny"), respectively.

In colloquial English each of the standard forms may be expressed in a variety of ways. Below is a list of sample translations into the more conventional language of the *A*-, *I*-, *O*-, and *E*-propositions.

Proposition	*Translation*
1. Any carrot is yellow	All carrots are yellow
2. Carrots are always yellow	" " " "
3. Only yellow things are carrots	" " " "
4. At least one carrot is yellow	Some carrots are yellow
5. Many carrots are yellow	" " " "
6. Most carrots are yellow	" " " "

Proposition	Translation
7. Carrots are sometimes yellow	" " " "
8. Carrots are rarely yellow	Some carrots are not yellow
9. Not all carrots are yellow	" " " " "
10. Carrots are never yellow	No carrots are yellow
11. All carrots are not yellow	Ambiguous. Means either 9 or 10, above

The third example above shows that "only" reverses the order of the subject and predicate in an *A* proposition. This is similar to the power of the same word to reverse the antecedent and consequent of a conditional proposition, as in "*p* only if *q*," which contrasts with "*p* if *q*." In general, "Only *S* is *P*" is called an *exclusive proposition*. Besides exclusive propositions there are *exceptive propositions,* exempliefid by "All except *S* is *P*." This translates into the *A*-proposition "All non-*S* is *P*."

Some of the standard forms themselves deserve further explanation. *I*, for example, should be taken to mean "At least one *S* is *P*; possibly all *S* are *P*." Thus *I* does not imply *O*; on our present interpretation, "Some Representatives are women" does not imply "Some Representatives are not women," since it does not rule out the truth of "All Representatives are women." And if only one Representative is a woman, the proposition to this effect will, on this interpretation, have *I* as its form.

It is important to notice that both *A* and *E*, as they stand, are somewhat ambiguous. The *A*-proposition would perhaps most frequently be regarded as meaning "All *S* is *P*—and there are *S*'s." Surely the statement "All whales are mammals" suggests that there are whales. But on the other hand, does "All children attending this performance will be accompanied by an adult" imply that there are any children attending this performance? And can the existence of giants be inferred from "All men over fifteen feet tall must stoop to pass under this railway trestle"? All, in fact, that is intended by these last two propositions is that *if* any entity should belong to the class denoted by the subject, *then* the predicate in question would apply to it, but possibly the subject denotes nothing existent. This reading of *A*-propositions is known as the *hypothetical* interpretation, while the supposition that the subject-class is not empty is the *existential* interpretation. Analogously, the *E* proposition can also be understood in each of these two ways. We shall shortly commit ourselves explicitly to one of these two possible interpretations of universal propositions. No such decision need be made, of course, in connection with particular propositions, for their existential import is clear.

On reason for distinguishing between the existential and hypothetical modes of interpretation is that certain connections of truth-value subsisting among the four standard forms will vary according to the interpretation chosen. On the hypothetical reading, if *A* is true, then *O* is false, but nothing follows regarding the truth or falsity of either *I* or *E*. But if the existential interpretation be adopted, then the truth of *A* implies the truth of *I* and the falsity of *E*, as well as the falsity of *O*. The reasons for all these differences will be made clear very shortly.

In general, the truth-functional relations of the standard propositions are represented by a *Square of Opposition*. For the *existential* interpretation, this square is as follows:

FIGURE 1

Contradictories, of course, are two propositions of which one must be true and the other false. And this relationship does indeed hold between *E* and *I*; for no *S* is *P* if, and only if, it is false that some *S* is *P*. Similarly, the truth-value of *A* is always the opposite of that of *O*. *Contraries,* it will be remembered, are propositions of which not both may be simultaneously true but both might well be false (see page 46). The example given in Section 7 illustrates this point: "All tomatoes are red" and "No tomatoes are red" could not both be true; in fact, both are false. When two propositions are *subcontraries,* both may be true but not both may be false; "Some *S* is *P*" and "Some *S* is not *P*," viewed existentially, afford examples. *Subalterns* are pairs of propositions such that the truth of one implies the truth of the other. If there are *S*'s, then obviously "All *S* is *P*" implies "Some *S* is *P*," and likewise *E* implies *O*.

To interpret the standard forms *hypothetically* is to blot out the perimeter of Figure 1. All that remains is the following weakened diagram:

FIGURE 2

To grasp this new set of relationships, let us consider various possible propositions about the contents of an empty bookshelf. To say "All of the books on the shelf are red" is exactly the same as to say "None of the books on the shelf is red," since there are no books. Thus *A* and *E* are in this case both true. And both *I* and *O* are false, since "Some of the books on the shelf are red" and "Some of the books on the shelf are not red" fail together when there are no books. Thus *A* and *E* are no longer contraries, and *I* and *O* are not subcontraries. And since the former are both true and the latter false, *A* cannot imply *I*, nor can *E* imply *O*; so there are no longer any subalterns.

Now consider the consequences of placing one book on the shelf. All the relationships of Figure 1 will be reinstated. Thus when no assumption is made regarding the content of *S*, each of the pairs of propositions peripheral to the Square of Opposition may involve any one of the possible assignments of truth-values. Therefore the propositions of each pair are independent.

EXERCISES

A. Which of the following arguments belong to the logic of propositions? Which to the logic of classes? Explain.

1. All trout are fish.
   All fish swim.
   ―――――――――
   All trout swim.
2. If Flossie is a trout, then Flossie is a fish.
   If Flossie is a fish, then Flossie swims.
   ―――――――――――――――――――――
   If Flossie is a trout, then Flossie swims.
3. It is not the case both that the bomb exploded and that no one was hurt. Therefore, either the bomb did not explode or it is false that no one was hurt.
4. No one was hurt. Therefore, everyone was unhurt.
5. Since it is false that no one was hurt, it follows that someone was hurt.
6. No giraffes ever shout. No one who shouts is well mannered. Therefore, all giraffes are well mannered.
7. If no one who shouts is well mannered, then Meggs is a boor.

But it is true that no one who shouts is well mannered. Therefore, Meggs *is* a boor.

8. $p \to q$
$q \to r$
$$p \to r$$

9. 7 is greater than 5
5 is greater than 2
7 is greater than 2

10. Either 7 is greater than 5, or 5 is greater than 7. But it is not the case that 5 is greater than 7. Therefore, 7 is greater than 5.

B. Express each of the following in subject–predicate form. Underline the subject once and the predicate twice.

(*Sample:* Boggs sleeps. Ans. Boggs is a sleeper or Boggs is a person who sleeps.)

1. Sugar is sweet.
2. Sucrose is sugar.
3. Diggs eats sugar.
4. Diggs enjoys eating sugar.
5. The body requires sugar.
6. Saccharin is sweeter than sugar.
7. Sugar is not an inorganic compound.
8. Whenever I drink coffee, I put sugar in it.
9. Virtue is its own reward.
10. The virtuous man will be rewarded.
11. Virtue is not easily attainable.
12. Patience is a virtue.
13. No one cares for virtue today.
14. Whoever advocates virtue today takes the chance of being considered a prude.
15. No animal can be regarded as truly virtuous.

D. Express each of the following as a proposition having one of the four standard forms.

(*Sample:* Only employees are allowed to park here. Ans. All people allowed to park here are employees. An *A*-proposition.)

1. Every mammal has hair.
2. Lizards never have hair.

3. Whoever reads his newspaper knows that the world is in a mess.
4. Whenever I read the newspaper, I feel depressed.
5. All but minors may vote.
6. None but members are eligible to use the squash courts.
7. There is at least one prime number between 20 and 30.
8. Each member of the squad receives a uniform.
9. Not all members of the squad receive letters.
10. Most members of the squad get a chance to play.
11. No one who appreciates the order of the universe can be an atheist.
12. Lincoln emancipated the slaves.
13. Gold is a metal.
14. Gold is rarely used as a medium of exchange.
15. All is not gold that glitters.

E. For each of the following pairs of propositions: (a) state the relationship between the propositions (contraries, contradictories, subalterns, or subcontraries); (b) supposing that the *first* member of the pair is *true,* decide whether the second member is *true, false,* or *indeterminate;* and (c) supposing that the *second* member of the pair is *false,* decide whether the first member is *true, false,* or *indeterminate.*

Assume the existential interpretation of universal propositions.

(*Sample:* (i) All tomatoes are red.   (ii) No tomatoes are red.   Ans. (a) Contraries.   (b) If (i) is true, then (ii) is false.   (c) If (ii) is false, then (i) is indeterminate.

1. (i) Some tomatoes are red.
   (ii) Some tomatoes are not red.
2. (i) All voters can read.
   (ii) Some voters can read.
3. (i) Some gases are heavier than air.
   (ii) No gases are heavier than air.
4. (i) No symphony by Haydn calls for a trombone.
   (ii) Some symphonies by Haydn do not call for trombones.
5. (i) No fish breathes air.
   (ii) Some fish breathe air.
6. (i) Some motion is not perpetual.
   (ii) No motion is perpetual.
7. (i) All events have causes.

    (ii) Some events do not have causes.
8. (i) Some vegetables grow under the ground.
    (ii) All vegetables grow under the ground.
9. (i) Only perfect squares have rational square roots.
    (ii) Some numbers with rational square roots are perfect squares.
10. (i) All except pass-holders must pay admission.
    (ii) Some non-pass-holders need not pay admission.
11. (i) All wars are caused by economic crises.
    (ii) No wars are caused by economic crises.
12. (i) None of the workers was hurt.
    (ii) All of the workers were hurt.
13. (i) Some swans are not white.
    (ii) All swans are white.
14. (i) Few Republicans are southern Governors.
    (ii) Many Republicans are southern Governors.
15. (i) It never rains but it pours.
    (ii) Whenever it rains, it pours.

F. Carry out the instructions for Exercise E, *assuming the hypothetical interpretation of universal propositions.*

SUPPLEMENTARY READINGS

1. Max Black, *Critical Thinking,* New York, Prentice-Hall, Inc., 2d ed., 1952, Ch. 7.

2. J. N. Keynes, *Studies and Exercises in Formal Logic,* London, Macmillan and Co., 4th ed., 1906, Pt. II, Ch. III.

3. W. Stanley Jevons, *Elementary Lessons in Logic,* London, Macmillan and Co., 1893, Lesson XI.

4. Monroe C. Beardsley, *Practical Logic,* New York, Prentice-Hall, Inc., 1950, Ch. 8.

13

Immediate Inference and Venn Diagrams

In this section we shall be concerned with arguments like 12.1 ("Some Representatives are women; therefore, some women are Representatives"). For our present purposes, any argument *is* like 12.1 provided (a) its variables are terms and (b) it contains just one premise. Another example of the arguments we shall now discuss is

(13.1) No fish is rational

All fish are nonrational,

since this argument also satisfies conditions (a) and (b) just given. Any argument like 12.1 and 13.1 is called an *immediate inference*. This is a general name for argument-structures of a certain type; in this respect it corresponds to "conditional argument," "alternative argument," and so on. But it is worth pointing out that "immediate inference," though traditional in usage, is somewhat of a misnomer. For *inference* is involved here to no greater extent than in any other argument. Arguments like 12.1 and 13.1 might with equal accuracy have been characterized as examples of "immediate *implication*." In any event, the sense in which implication, or inference, is *immediate* here, rather than non-immediate, will become clear when we begin to study the syllogism.

A general method for testing the validity of immediate inferences is known as *Venn Diagrams,* after the nineteenth-century

English logician John Venn. A Venn Diagram portrays a given relation between the subject and predicate of a proposition in such a way that whatever other relations there may also be between the two terms in question can be directly read from the diagram. All of the relations envisaged by the traditional analysis of propositions are, in Venn Diagrams, represented as qualifications of a fixed pattern of two intersecting circles, one representing the subject, and the other the predicate, of the proposition under consideration. The num-

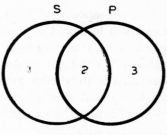

FIGURE 3

bers 1, 2, and 3 denote different parts of *S* and *P*. Thus 1 is that part of *S* which is not *P*, 3 is that part of *P* which is not *S*, and 2 is whatever is common to *S* and *P*. If *S* is *tomatoes* and *P* is *red things*, then 1 means "tomatoes which are not red," 3 means "red things which are not tomatoes," and 2 means "red tomatoes." But it is well to remember that Figure 3, as it stands, ascribes no particular relation to *S* and *P*; *it is simply the basic pattern common to all Venn Diagrams.* In order to express a particular

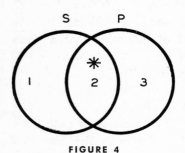

FIGURE 4

relation—say, that involved in the *A*-proposition "All tomatoes are red," or the *O*-proposition "Some tomatoes are not red"—further symbols are needed. One such symbol is the star (*). When this star is placed in one or another of the three areas of Figure 3, it indicates *that the portion of S or P which is starred applies to at least one object.* Consider, for example, the effect of putting a star in area 2. The meaning of Figure 4 is, then, that Area 2— whatever is common to *S* and *P*—applies to at least one object. Thus, for example, "red tomatoes" applies to at least one object.

But this is just an abstract way of saying "At least one tomato is red." And this, in turn, is exactly the *I*-proposition "Some tomatoes are red." So in general, Figure 4 represents the *I*-proposition "Some *S* is *P*."

The *O*-proposition "Some *S* is not *P*" may be expressed by putting a star in area 1 of Figure 3; for this means, "That part of *S* which is not *P* applies to at least one object" or, in other words, "Some *S* is not *P*." Notice that the star in area 1 conveys no information as to whether area 2 is similarly starred, thus reflecting the interpretation of the word "some" which we have adopted. "Some *S* is not *P*" does not imply "Some *S* is *P*," for it is perfectly compatible with "No *S* is *P*."

The effect of starring area 3 is to express the proposition "Some *P* is not *S*." The relationship between this proposition and "Some *S* is not *P*" will be discussed shortly; in the meantime it will be obvious that the two propositions do not have the same meaning. For the moment, let us consider what we have accomplished so far in the effort to symbolize propositions having each of the standard forms. We have succeeded in representing diagrammatically each of the two *particular* propositions *I* and *O*. But we have as yet no device for qualifying our basic pattern of two intersecting circles so as to express the *universal* propositions *A* and *E*.

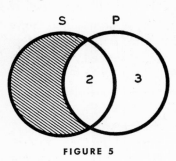

FIGURE 5

This need is satisfied by the method of indicating that a given area of Figure 3 *applies to no objects at all*. To indicate this, we shall shade the area in question, as in the following figure. The shading in Figure 5 operates to cancel out area 1—to express the idea that there is no *S* which is not *P*. Thus whatever *S* there is must fall wholly within *P*. If *S* is *tomatoes* and *P* is *red things,* then Figure 5 asserts "If anything is a tomato, it is red." But it does not assert that there *are* any tomatoes or red things, since it involves no starred areas.   What is expresses is thus just the *A*-proposition "All *S* is *P*," *assuming the hypothetical interpretation of universal proposi- tions.*   In general, Figure 5 assumes the hypothetical interpretation because it means only "If area 2 applies to any object, then area 3 also applies to it."   But the assumption that area 2 does apply to any object is not represented here; in effect, Figure 5 involves no commitment to the *existential* interpretation of universal propo- sitions.

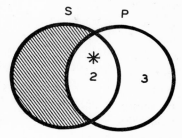

FIGURE 6

This is not to suggest that Venn Diagrams are incapable of expressing the existential interpretation. In order to convey the idea that area 2 is not empty, it is sufficient to combine Figures 4 and 5.   This diagram means not only that *if* anything is *S,* it is P, but also that something *is S.   From now on, however, we shall commit ourselves explicitly to the hypothetical interpretation,* and will not draw composite diagrams like Figure 6 in analyzing immediate inference.   From the point of view of the systematic organization of this book, the hypothetical interpreta- tion has several decided advantages over the existential.   Not that

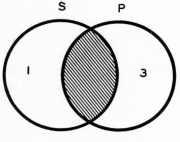

FIGURE 7

it is "true" while the other is "false"; there is clearly no way of discovering which interpreta- tion is abstractly true.   And a diagram is true or false only rela- tively to a given interpretation of universal propositions.

The *E*-proposition "No *S* is *P*," which like A is universal, requires some shading in the basic pattern of two intersecting circles.   And it is not difficult to see which area should be shaded.   If *S* is *tomatoes* and *P* is *red things*, then the effect of Figure 7 is to cancel out the possibility of objects which are both tomatoes and red things. But this is precisely to say "No tomatoes are red." The hypothetical interpretation is assumed in Figure 7; in order to represent an *E*-proposition interpreted existentially, we should also need a star in area 1 to indicate the existence of at least one object to which *S* applies. But the hypothetical interpretation, which does not require this star, is, as we have said, to be our standard assumption from now on.

To make use of Venn Diagrams in testing the validity of various sorts of immediate inference, we have only to reflect that *if two propositions have the same meaning, they must yield the same diagram.* Consider the two propositions "Some Representatives are women" and "Some women are Representatives." These yield, respectively, Figure 8 and Figure 9.

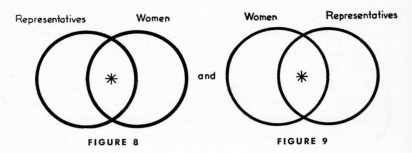

FIGURE 8   FIGURE 9

Now the only difference between these drawings is one of spatial orientation; Figure 9 is, in effect, Figure 8 seen from behind. But such distinctions are of no more concern here than they are, say, in plane geometry; neither a Venn Diagram nor a Euclidean triangle is defined in terms of its position in space. In particular, Venn Diagrams are defined only as an abstract relation between two specifically identified intersecting circles and a shading or star, and in this sense Figures 8 and 9 portray exactly the same relation. We may conclude, then, that "Some Representatives are women" does have the same meaning as "Some women are Representatives," and that the two propositions are *equivalent.* But when *p* is equivalent to *q* ("*p* ← → *q*"), this entails that *p implies q,* since "$p \leftarrow \rightarrow q$" was defined in Section 9 (page 68) as "$(p \rightarrow q)$ & $(q \rightarrow p)$." Therefore 12.1, an argument having "Some Representatives are women" as a premise and "Some women are Representatives" as a conclusion, is *valid*—any argument is valid if its conclusion is in reality implied by its premise or premises. Where the conclusion is *equivalent* to the premise, the case for validity is simply stronger, in the sense that the argument would still be valid if its premise and conclusion were interchanged.

A contrasting case is that of any argument such as

(13.2) All humans are rational beings.
 All rational beings are humans.

Using Figure 5 as a model, and labeling the appropriate circle *H* for "humans" and *R* for "rational beings," we obtain two diagrams, one corresponding to the premise and the other to the conclusion:

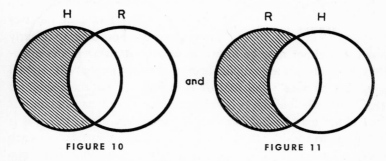

FIGURE 10   FIGURE 11

Now Figures 10 and 11, unlike Figures 8 and 9, are not the same, and no readjustment of their spatial positions could make them identical. It is an irreducible fact that "*H* but not *R*" is shaded in Figure 10, while "*R* but not *H*" is shaded in Figure 11. Assuming that if two propositions yield different diagrams, they must have different meanings, we may infer that the premise of 13.2 does not mean what its conclusion does.

This does not, of course, establish as yet that 13.2 is *invalid;* for one proposition may *imply* another even when they have different meanings. But the premise of 13.2 does not, in fact, imply its conclusion.   For when $p \to q$, p cannot be true unless q is true, and thus if p and q can properly be represented in terms of Venn Diagrams, it will be impossible to diagram p without automatically representing q.   This happens, for example, in the case of the A-proposition and the I-proposition when the existential interpretation is adopted, since it is impossible to draw Figure 6 without at the same time drawing Figure 4.   Thus $A \to I$, which is another way of stating that A and I are, on the existential interpretation, *subalterns* (see Figure 1 on page 108).

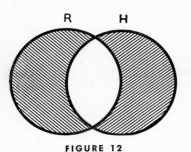

R   H

FIGURE 12

It is, however, quite possible to diagram "All humans are rational beings" without automatically representing "All rational beings are humans." One way of showing this is to draw them both on the same diagram.   The fact that the two shadings do not overlap clearly shows that either may be drawn in without drawing in the other. Thus, "All humans are rational beings" does not imply "All rational beings are humans"; and so 13.2 is invalid.   How, then, shall we regard the relationship between its premise and its conclusion? Since either may be *diagrammed* independently of the other, it is reasonable to consider the two *propositions* as independent of each other, in the sense that *neither implies the other*.   In general, two propositions are independent when both may be represented, without overlapping or interference, upon the same basic Venn-Diagram pattern.

The possibility that two diagrams might *interfere* with each other deserves some comment.   Interference would occur whenever one attempted to represent both a given proposition and its contradictory upon the same pair of intersecting circles.   Consider "All tomatoes are red" and "Some tomatoes are not red."   Together, these two propositions yield Figure 13.   It is impossible, however, to interpret this diagram. For the star means that there is at least one object to which the designation "Tomatoes which are not red things" applies, while the shading means that there is no such object at all. This diagram thus falls beyond the pale of logic; it is symptomatic of a fundamental incongruity. Wherever we find it, we may be sure that the propositions represented are *inconsistent* with each other.

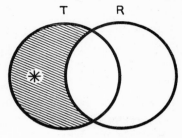

FIGURE 13

Let us summarize the results of the last few pages. Where *p* and *q* are propositions in subject–predicate form:

(a) *P* and *q* have the *same* diagram if, and only if, they are *equivalent*.

(b) The diagram of *p* automatically includes the diagram of *q* if, and only if, "*p* implies *q*."

(c) *P* and *q* can be diagrammed on the same basic pair of intersecting circles without overlapping or interfering if, and only if, *p* and *q* are *independent*.

(d) The diagram of *p* interferes with the diagram of *q* if, and only if, *p* and *q* are *inconsistent*.

The notions of *equivalence, independence,* and *inconsistency* here are the same as in Section 7 (page 45), where it was pointed out that a given *conditional* proposition is *equivalent* to its contrapositive, *independent* of its converse, and *inconsistent* with (the *contradictory* of) its contradictory. A conditional proposition is not, of course, to be confused with the simple propositions we are now dealing with. Conditional propositions are always complex, having propositional constituents in the form of antecedent and consequent. But what we are discussing now are simple propositions analyzed into the nouns or adjectives which we are calling "subject" and "predicate." The relevance of the notions of equivalence, independence, and inconsistency to propositions of both of these basic types shows that these notions are themselves more fundamental than the distinction between the logic of propositions and the logic of classes. They will turn up again in Part Four, where we shall study them as ideas in their own right, and will be concerned with some of the ways in which they are related to each other.

Let us now attempt to systematize the results of applying Venn Diagrams to problems of immediate inference. We have found that "Some Representatives are women, therefore some women are Representatives" is valid, but that "All humans are rational beings, therefore all rational beings are humans" is invalid. This suggests the general question "Under what conditions can we validly argue from a given premise to a conclusion in which the subject and the predicate of the premise are exchanged for each other?" In general, where the premise is an *I*-proposition, we can, but where it is an *A*-proposition, we cannot. What of the *E*- and the *O*-propositions? Consider in the first place

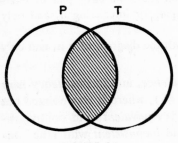

FIGURE 14

(13.3) No pigs are tidy.
No tidy beings are pigs.

Both the premise and the conclusion of 13.3 yield the same diagram, as Figure 14 shows. (Here we adopt the convenient procedure of labeling the two circles with the initial letters of the subject and predicate respectively). We may conclude that 13.3 is valid, and that in general "No *S* is *P*, therefore no *P* is *S*" would be valid.

Finally, no argument of the form "Some *S* is not *P*, therefore some *P* is not *S*" is valid. For example, where *S* is *tomatoes* and *P* is *red things,* both the premise and the conclusion can be represented on the same diagram without overlapping or interference. This result may seem odd. For surely the premise "Some tomatoes are not red" and the conclusion "Some red things are not tomatoes" are both true. But the reader who experiences doubt is referred to the discussion of truth and validity in Section 6 (pages 31-35). An invalid argument, as well as a valid one, may have all true premises and a true conclusion. The distinction between the two sorts of argument lies only in the fact that a valid argument cannot have all true premises but a false conclu-

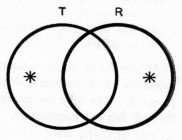

FIGURE 15

sion, whereas an invalid argument can. To show that an argument having exactly the same form as "Some tomatoes are not red, therefore some red things are not tomatoes" might have true premise and false conclusion, we need only find appropriate substitutions for "tomatoes" and "red things," as in

(13.4) Some vegetables are not tomatoes.
_____
Some tomatoes are not vegetables.

The conclusions reached so far with respect to immediate inference may be summarized in terms of the idea of *converse* of a proposition in standard form. This idea is to be sharply distinguished from that of the converse of a *conditional* proposition discussed in Section 7 (page 44). The latter idea is involved in the logic of propositions, but the sense of "converse" which we are now about to define occurs only within that area of logic in which propositions themselves are analyzed into their constituent parts. In this sense, *the converse of a given proposition is the result of exchanging its subject with its predicate.* Thus the converse of "All S is P" is "All P is S," that of "Some S is P" is "Some P is S," that of "Some S is not P" is "Some P is not S," and that of "No S is P" is "No P is S." We may summarize by saying

(a) The *A*-proposition is not equivalent to its converse. (This is sometimes expressed by saying that it "does not convert.")

(b) The *I*-proposition is equivalent to its converse. (It "converts.")

(c) The *O*-proposition is not equivalent to its converse. (It "does not convert.")

(d) The *E*-proposition is equivalent to its converse. (It "converts.")

At this point we have successfully analyzed all but one of the examples of immediate inference which we have so far brought forward. The lone exception is 13.1, "No fish is rational, therefore all fish are nonrational." And this argument is still opaque to our analysis, since its conclusion is not the converse of its premise. Indeed, the premise and the conclusion are related in a manner which is at the moment quite unfamiliar. Let us define this relationship, and then determine to what extent Venn Diagrams would be useful in testing the validity of those immediate inferences in which premise and conclusion are so related.

The conclusion of 13.1 is the *obverse* of its premise. In general, one may transform a proposition in standard form into its obverse by changing the proposition as a whole from affirmative to negative or negative to affirmative and at the same time putting the prefix "non-" (or an equivalent prefix) before its predicate. Neither the subject of the proposition nor its status as universal or particular is altered in any way. For each of the standard forms, the effect of this procedure is as follows:

(a) The obverse of "All *S* is *P*" is "No *S* is *non-P*."

(b) The obverse of "Some *S* is *P*" is "Some *S* is not *non-P*."

(c) The obverse of "Some *S* is not *P*" is "Some *S* is *non-P*."

(d) The obverse of "No *S* is *P*" is "All *S* is *non-P*."

Since the results of forming the obverse of the *I*- and of the *O*-propositions are somewhat trivial, we shall not discuss these forms any further in this context. The problem now is to determine whether the *A* is *equivalent* with its obverse, and likewise for the *E*. Since it is not generally true that a proposition is equivalent to its *converse*, there is no reason to suspect, in advance of analysis, that any given proposition would be equivalent to its *obverse*. The analysis needed here is again provided by Venn Diagrams.

Let us recall the considerations which guided us in constructing Figure 5, a diagram for the *A*-proposition "All *S* is *P*." We wanted to indicate that whatever object *S* applies to falls wholly within the *P*-circle. To this end, we shaded out area 1. But the effect of this shading is no more than to assert that there is *no* object to which the designation "*S* but *non-P*" would apply; or, in other words, "No *S* is *non-P*." In the very process of diagramming the *A*-proposition we have also diagrammed this, its obverse. And since it *is* the obverse of the *A*, it follows that *A and its obverse are equivalent*.

The relation between *E* and its obverse can be similarly exhibited. Figure 7, which represents the former, says that nothing is common to *S* and *P*. But in the act of conveying this information it also shows that any occupant of area 1 would be excluded from *P*; whatever *S* there is must necessarily be *non-P*. Thus all *S* is *non-P*; but this is the obverse of *E*. So *E and its obverse are equivalent*. By virtue of this equivalence, immediate inferences like 13.1 are valid. A further example is

(13.5) No pigs are tidy.
_____
All pigs are untidy.

We have dealt so far with *conversion,* in which neither the subject nor the predicate of a proposition is changed from an affirmative to a negative form, and with *obversion,* where the predicate is so changed by prefixing it with "non-." No method has as yet been provided for transforming a proposition into an equivalent form in which the *subject* is preceded by "non-." And as a matter of fact there is no such method in general. For "All *non-S* is *P*" is independent of any proposition we have analyzed in this section. And the same is true of "Some *non-S* is not *P*."

In order to show this, however, we need to revise the pattern basic to Venn Diagrams. For while there is a place on our diagram for "*non-S* which is *P*"—namely, area 3 of Figure 3—we have as yet no way of representing "*non-S* which is *not P*." But we shall need such an additional area in order to diagram "All *non-S* is *P*," since, on the principles we have adopted, this involves canceling out all the *non-S* which is not *P*.

The additional area needed is located in a rectangle framing the basic intersecting circles and representing what is known as the *universe of discourse*. This "universe" is the class of all objects within which it is significant to distinguish between *S* and *non-S*. For example if *S* is *Americans* and *non-S non-Americans,* the intended universe of discourse is likely to be *people,* since it is not likely to be significant to distinguish Americans from *everything*

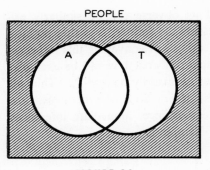

PEOPLE

FIGURE 16

which is not an American—not only European and Asian people, but also sticks, stones, and triangles. To say that all non-Americans are thrifty, for example, is not to say that equilateral triangles are thrifty. According to the description just given, we must diagram "All non-Americans are thrifty" as shown at the left.

The shaded area in Figure 16 represents *non-Americans who are not thrifty.* And the effect of the shading is to cancel out this area—to say, in other words, that all non-Americans are confined to the *T* circle and that they are all thrifty. Figure 16 bears out the previous remark to the effect that "all *non-S* is *P*" is independent of any proposition we have hitherto analyzed. For within the remaining empty circles it would still be possible to diagram any of the standard propositions.

"Some *non-S* is not *P*" is likewise independent of all of the standard forms and their converses and obverses. Consider, for example, "Some non-mammals are not oviparous." Here the universe of discourse is *animals*. The star indicates that the area representing *non-mammals which are not oviparous* applies to at least one object.

The remaining forms having negative subjects, namely, "Some *non-S* is *P*" and "No *non-S* is *P*," do not require to be diagrammed within a universe of discourse, since the former is the converse of the standard *O*-proposition and the latter has, as can readily be shown by obversion, exactly the same meaning as the converse of the standard *A*.

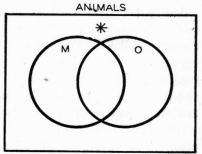

ANIMALS

FIGURE 17

These propositions may be easily portrayed on the basic pattern originally adopted.

Only one other form related to those so far discussed is of interest: the result of exchanging the subject and predicate of a given proposition *and* placing "non-" before each. This form is known as the *contrapositive* of the given proposition, and, as in the case of the converse, is not to be confused with the contrapositive of a *conditional*. The contrapositive of "All *S* is *P*" is thus "All *non-P* is *non-S*," and the contrapositive of "No *S* is *P*" is "No *non-P* is *non-S*." It is not necessary to deal with the contrapositives of *I*- and *O*-propositions.

As before, we must ask: "Is the contrapositive of a given proposition equivalent with it?" Perhaps the simplest way to answer this question is to consider how the contrapositive is related to the converse and the obverse, rather than to consult Venn Diagrams directly. For the contrapositive of any proposition is formed from it by a series of steps involving conversion and obversion. In particular, it is derived by first obverting the proposition, then converting the result, and then obverting that result. If we begin with *A*, for example, we shall obtain first "No *S* is *non-P*," then "No *non-P* is *S*," and finally, "All *non-P* is *non-S*." And since each step is a passage from one proposition to another which is equivalent to it, we may conclude that *the A-proposition is equivalent to its contrapositive.*

Let us determine whether *E* is also equivalent to its contrapositive. The obverse of "No *S* is *P*" is "All *S* is *non-P*," and the converse of that is "All *non-P* is *S*." By obversion we would be led to "No *non-P* is *non-S*," the contrapositive in question. But this chain has a defective link. For the converse of "All *S* is *non-P*"—an *A*-proposition—is not equivalent with it. It follows that the *E-proposition is not equivalent with its contrapositive.*

Thus one further form of immediate inference—where the premise is an *A*-proposition and the conclusion its contrapositive— is vindicated. An example is

(13.6)   All squares are rectangles.

All non-rectangles are non-squares.

EXERCISES

A. Draw a Venn Diagram for each of the propositions listed in Exercise D following Section 12 (pages 111-12).

B. (a) Use Venn Diagrams to verify each of the relationships exhibited in the Square of Opposition for the *hypothetical* interpretation of universal propositions (Figure 2, page 109). In other words, prove that the members of each pair of propositions around the perimeter of this square are independent, and that the propositions at opposite end of diagonals are contradictories. (b) Explain the diagram which shows that *A* and *E* are independent. Can *S* apply to any object when *A* and *E* are both true? How is this connected with the fact that one has adopted the hypothetical interpretation?

C. Supposing that *all Mohammedans are nondrinkers,* determine whether each of the following is *equivalent* to this, *independent* of it, or *inconsistent* with it.

  1. Some Mohammedans are drinkers.
  2. No Mohammedans are drinkers.

3. Some drinkers are Mohammedans.
4. Some drinkers are not Mohammedans.
5. All non-Mohammedans are drinkers.
6. All non-drinkers are Mohammedans.
7. All drinkers are non-Mohammedans.
8. Drinkers are never Mohammedans.
9. Non-Mohammedans are always non-drinkers.
10. Non-drinkers are never non-Mohammedans.

D. Supposing that *some immoral people are happy,* determine whether each of the following is *equivalent* to this, *independent* of it, or *inconsistent* with it.

1. Some immoral people are unhappy.
2. All immoral people are happy.
3. No immoral people are happy.
4. Some happy people are immoral.
5. Some happy people are not moral.
6. All happy people are moral.
7. Some unhappy people are moral.
8. Most immoral people are unhappy.
9. No happy people are immoral.
10. All immoral people are unhappy.

E. Making use of the valid forms of immediate inference, and, where necessary, the Square of Opposition for the hypothetical interpretation, determine whether each of the following arguments is valid. In each case, indicate the relation, if any, between the premise and conclusion (for example, converse, obverse, and so forth).

1. All giants are over ten feet tall.

   All creatures over ten feet tall are giants.
2. No giants are less than ten feet tall.

   No creatures less than ten feet tall are giants.
3. Only giants are over ten feet tall.

   All non-giants are creatures not over ten feet tall.
4. No engineer has invented a perpetual-motion machine.

   Some non-engineers have invented a perpetual-motion machine.
5. All men over ten feet tall are giants.

   Some men over ten feet tall are giants.

6. No incompetent worker is worthy of praise.

   No worker unworthy of praise is competent.

7. Some mammals lay eggs.

   It is false that no mammals lay eggs.

8. All humans are mortal.

   All immortals are nonhuman.

9. All arguments with premises all true and conclusion false are invalid.

   No arguments with premises all true and conclusion false are valid.

10. Some arguments belong to the logic of propositions.

    Some arguments do not belong to the logic of propositions.

11. All valid arguments are logical truths.

    All invalid arguments are logical falsehoods.

12. Whoever sits on this chair will get a surprise.

    Nobody who sits on this chair will fail to get a surprise.

13. It is not the case that all dollar alarm clocks keep perfect time.

    No dollar alarm clocks keep perfect time.

14. Some rich men are not generous.

    Some generous men are not rich.

15. No priest is married.

    All priests are unmarried.

SUPPLEMENTARY READINGS

1. Alice Ambrose and Morris Lazerowitz, *Fundamentals of Symbolic Logic,* New York, Rinehart & Company, Inc., 1948, Ch. X.

2. Monroe C. Beardsley, *Practical Logic,* New York, Prentice-Hall, Inc., 1950, Ch. 9.

14

Venn Diagrams for the Syllogism

The sense in which immediate inference is "immediate" is that its premise leads directly to its conclusion without any intervening steps. Non-immediate, or *mediate* inference (to use the traditional terminology) would, on the other hand, require a further link between premise and conclusion. An example of mediate inference is

(14.1) Some Representatives are women.
        All Representatives are over twenty-one.
        _____
        Some people over twenty-one are women.

Here "All Representatives are over twenty-one" is the connecting link between the premise "Some Representatives are women" and the conclusion. From our point of view there is no reason for not regarding this link as a premise in its own right; it certainly conforms with all that we have said in general about premises. But we shall find it convenient to follow traditional usage in referring to this premise as the *minor* premise. The *major* premise is thus the one which appears first in 14.1. Technically, *the minor premise contains the subject of the conclusion, and the major premise contains the predicate of the conclusion.*

   While 14.1 may quite properly be called a "mediate inference," a much more common name for it, both in traditional and contemporary parlance, is *syllogism*—more accurately, perhaps, *cate-*

gorical syllogism. The qualification "categorical" is used when confusion between arguments such as 14.1 and chain arguments ("hypothetical syllogisms") is likely. But it is not likely that the reader of this book will confuse the syllogism with the chain argument, since the one falls within the logic of classes, while the other belongs strictly to the logic of propositions. In particular, *the syllogism is that sort of argument in the logic of classes the two premises of which contain three terms altogether, only two of which appear in its conclusion.* The only real resemblance it has to a chain argument is, then, that the conclusion expresses the elimination of something from the premises. But in one case, what is eliminated is a proposition, and in the other a term. And there are further differences between a syllogism and a chain argument. The latter may have any number of premises, while the former may have no more than two. And we shall soon see that most syllogisms are far more complex than chain arguments.

Clearly, 14.1 is a valid argument, but there are others which pose a problem. For example,

(14.2) All who wear spats wear frock coats.
        No baboons wear spats.
        ───────────────────────────────
        No baboons wear frock coats.

That 14.2 is in fact invalid may be ascertained by substituting "reptiles" for the term "[those] who wear spats" and "have two eyes" for "wear frock coats." But to find such crucial substitutions is only a matter of intuition or luck, and could at best prove a given argument invalid but could never conclusively establish the validity of a valid argument. We need a general technique for determining whether any syllogism is valid or invalid.

There are actually at least four general methods for testing syllogisms. The first involves the employment of Venn Diagrams, the second makes use of a set of simple rules, the third refers to what is known as an *antilogism,* and the fourth is the method of *reduction to the first figure*—this last-named a method central to the earliest investigation of the syllogism by Aristotle. Since we shall not develop either of these last two methods in this book, it is irrelevant to define them or discuss them further now. But it does seem advantageous to expound both of the first two methods. Thus in the present section we shall consider the application of Venn Diagrams to the problem of distinguishing valid from invalid syllogisms, and in Section 15 we shall attempt to show how the same problem may be solved by means of a set of rules.

Immediate inference is an expression of the relationships existing between two classes—the terms of the premise and conclusion. Venn Diagrams consisting of two intersecting circles are adequate to analyze these relationships, because this basic pattern is capable of accounting for all the ways in which, according to traditional logic, two classes can be related. Now the syllogism expresses a relation among three classes, taken two at a time. Accordingly, we should expect to find three circles instead of two. And these three circles must intersect in such a way that the relationship asserted by the syllogism to exist between any pair of them can be exhibited in terms of an appropriate marking. The basic pattern is, thus, Figure 18.

M

S   P

FIGURE 18

Here *S* denotes the subject of the conclusion (called the *minor term,* because it also occurs in the minor premise), *P*, the predicate of the conclusion (the *major term*), and *M*, the term which appears in the premises but not in the conclusion (the *middle term*). Figure 18 is, in effect, three basic Venn Diagram patterns fused into one. Reading clockwise, we see first, a pattern in which the relationship between *M* and *P* may be represented; then one for *P* and *S*; and finally one for *S* and *M*.

In order to test whether a given syllogism is valid we have only to diagram each of the premises in the part of pattern which corresponds to it. Then, *if in the process of diagramming the premises we have automatically diagrammed the conclusion, the syllo-*

gism is valid; otherwise, it is not.   This criterion follows from a statement made in Section 13: "The diagram of *p* automatically includes the diagram of *q* if, and only if, *p implies q*."   Thus if the diagram of the premises automatically includes that of the conclusion, the premises imply the conclusion.   And when the premises of any argument imply its conclusion, the argument is valid.

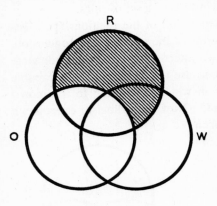

"All Representatives are over twenty-one."

FIGURE 19

Let us put 14.1 to this test. Using *R* for "Representatives," *W* for "women," and *O* for "people over twenty-one," we proceed to label the three intersecting circles. For reasons shortly to be discussed, we shall in this case diagram the minor premise of this argument first.   The result at this stage is Figure 19. Notice that the shading of the *R*-circle overlaps part of the *W*-circle.   We are at the moment ignoring *W* entirely—it need not concern us, since it does not occur at all in the minor premise. The *W* one sees in Figure 19 is "unreal"—a ghostly image which becomes embodied only in the next step, and cannot interfere with this one.

All that is now left for us to do is to portray the major premise. This means that we shall have to put a star somewhere in the area common to *R* and *W*.   There would seem to be two choices: either the star falls within *O*, as well as within *R* and *W*, or it falls outside *O*, in the shaded portion of *W*.   But in Section 13 it was emphasized that no area can be both starred and shaded at the same time; this would be a contradiction.   Therefore the star belongs in that part of the area common to *R* and *W* which is *not* shaded.

We have only to ask whether the conclusion "Some people over twenty-one are women," automatically appears. And it obviously does, since a star occurs in the area common to O and W.

Why did we begin with the minor premise, instead of turning directly to the major? The answer is that without the shading it would be impossible to tell where to place the star required by the major premise. And it is essential to know in precisely what portion of the area common to R and W the star properly belongs. If it had been possible to put the star in that part of W which, in Figure 20, is shaded, the conclusion "Some people over

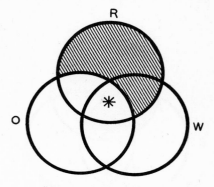

"Some Representatives are Women.
All Representatives are over twenty-one."

FIGURE 20

twenty-one are women" would not have followed, since in that area there would have been no indication of anything common to both

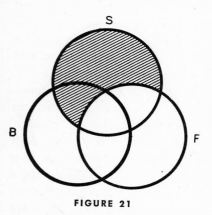

FIGURE 21

W and O. In general, we must adopt the rule: *Shade first, then star*, or *Diagram universal propositions before particular ones.*

Now let us apply the Venn Diagram test to 14.2, to see how its invalidity will be exhibited. Let S be "wearers of spats," let F be "wearers of frock coats," and let B be "baboons." The major premise may be diagrammed as in Figure 21. The shading required by the minor premise "No ba-

boons wear spats" is, in the process of portraying the major premise, already half-finished for us.   To complete the job, all that we
have to do is finish shading the area common to baboons and those

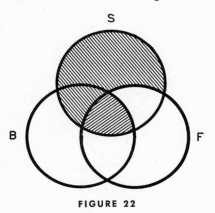

FIGURE 22

who wear spats.   But what
does this tell us about the
relation between *B* and *F*?
Nothing.   For in the remaining untouched parts of these
circles any of the four standard propositions, with *B* as the
subject and *F* as the predicate, could still consistently
be diagrammed.   But premises which are consistent with
any conclusion imply no conclusion.   "No baboons wear
frock coats," like all the other possibilities, is actually independent
of the premises which are supposed to imply it, and so the argument
is invalid.

The next figure shows the diagrams of two valid syllogisms.

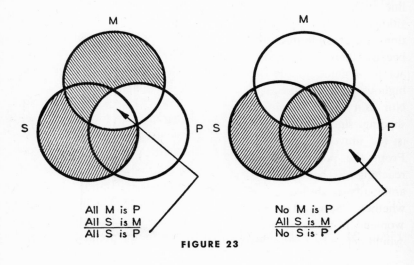

All M is P
All S is M
All S is P

No M is P
All S is M
No S is P

FIGURE 23

In each case the shading contributed by the major premise is distinguished from that associated with the minor premise through the use of lines running in different directions. Each arrow points to the area of the diagram in question where the conclusion may be read off. In the drawing on the left, successive shadings applied to the *S* circle have so shrunk the region of objects to which that circle can apply that all these objects now fall within the *P* circle; thus, "All *S* is *P*." On the right, successive shadings of the lens-shaped area common to *S* and *P* have canceled it out entirely; therefore, "No *S* is *P*."

There are several different symptoms of invalidity. One occurs in Figure 22; it is the case in which the act of diagramming the premises does not automatically result in a diagram of the conclusion. But sometimes it is impossible even to diagram the premises, as in

(14.3) Some Representatives are women.
        Some Representatives are Texans.
        _____
        Some Texans are women.

Figure 24 demonstrates the difficulty here. Each of the dotted lines indicates two possible positions of a star. Both positions are possible in each case because there is no shading to act as a guide to the unambiguous placement of the star. Nor can there be any such shading, since neither premise is a universal proposition. From the point of view of reaching a conclusion, this ambiguity is disastrous. For whether "Some Texans are

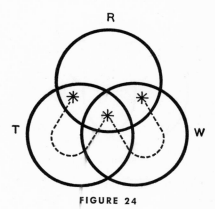

FIGURE 24

women" is to be regarded as automatically diagrammed or not would depend on which choice we arbitrarily made as to the proper place of each of the two stars.   If, for example, we decided on the left-hand star and the right-hand one, but ignored the one in the middle, the conclusions in question would fail to appear.   But it would appear for other selections.

A corollary of what has just been said is that in general, *two particular premises yield no conclusion;* for some shading is always required.   This rule will play an important part in the next section.

A third symptom of invalidity is that exhibited by a diagram which, while showing an unambiguous conclusion drawn in as the result of portraying the premises, still does not show the conclusion claimed by the syllogism under examination.   For instance

(14.4)   Some Representatives are women.
             No Representatives are under twenty-one.
             _____
             Some people under twenty-one are not women.

The requisite diagram appears below.

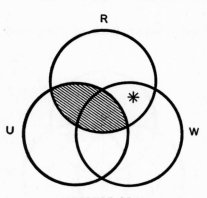

FIGURE 25

The star in Figure 25 serves to indicate that some occupants of the "*W*" circle fall outside the "*U*" circle—that some women are not under twenty-one.   But it does not indicate that some people under twenty-one are not women.   So 14.4 is, as it stands, invalid.

Any syllogism may be tested by means of Venn Diagrams. But syllogisms have many different forms; they vary widely both in the arrangement of terms and in the particular standard forms which characterize their premises and conclusions.   It would be tedious to have to use Venn Diagrams to test every possible type of syllogism for validity.   However, this task can readily be accomplished through the use of a simple set of rules. To these rules we now turn.

EXERCISE

Use Venn Diagrams to test the validity of each of the following syllogisms. Use the symbols suggested. (Numbers 1-7 are the same as in Exercise A following Section 6 (pages 35-36). The reader who did this earlier exercise is thus given the opportunity to justify his common-sense decisions regarding these arguments.)

1. All fish swim.
   All trout swim.

   All trout are fish.　　(F,S,T)
2. All fish swim.
   All trout are fish.

   All trout swim.　　(F,S,T)
3. All fish fly.
   All trout are fish.

   All trout fly.　　(Fi,Fl,T)
4. All fish fly.
   All trout fly.

   All trout are fish.　　(Fi,Fl,T)
5. All fish fly.
   All trout fly.

   All fish are trout.　　(Fi,Fl,T)
6. All fish fly.
   All robins are fish.

   All robins fly.　　(Fi,Fl,R)
7. All fish swim.
   All trout swim.

   All fish are trout.　　(F,S,T)
8. All thrushes are birds.
   No thrush is a lizard.

   No lizards are birds.　　(T,B,L)
9. No pig is a doctor.
   Some pigs are indelicate.

   Some indelicate creatures are not doctors.　　(P,D,I)

10. No pig is intelligent.
    No elephant is unintelligent.
    ___
    No elephant is a pig.   (P,I,E)
    (*Hint:* Obvert the minor premise.)

11. No square is nonrectangular.
    No rectangle has an angle-sum of 180 degrees.
    ___
    Anything having an angle-sum of 180 degrees is a non-square.
    (S,R,A)
    (*Hint:* Begin by using immediate inference to eliminate nega-
    tive terms.)

12. Some European automobiles do not have rear-wheel drive.
    All American automobiles have rear-wheel drive.
    ___
    Some American automobiles are not European automobiles.
    (E,R,A)

13. No liquid is a solid.
    No gas is a solid.
    ___
    No liquid is a gas.   (L,S,G)

14. Some swans are not white.
    All swans are birds.
    ___
    Some birds are not white.   (S,W,B)

15. All swans found in Europe are white.
    Some swans found in Australia are not white.
    ___
    Some swans found in Australia are not found in Europe.
    (E,W,A)

16. Some swans found in Australia are not white.
    All swans found in Europe are white.
    ___
    Some swans found in Europe are not found in Australia.
    (E,W,A)

17. All swans are birds.
    Some swans are not white.
    ___
    Some white creatures are not birds.   (S,B,W)

18. All round squares are round.
    All round squares are square.
    ___
    Some squares are round.   (RS,R,S)

19. No square is round.
    Some round things are wheels.
    ___
    Some wheels are not square.   (S,R,W)

20. Some wheels are not circular.
    All circular things roll.
    ___
    Some rolling things are not wheels.   (W,C,R)

21. All immoral people are unhappy.
Some unhappy people do not feel secure.
Some people who feel secure are moral.   (I,U,S)

22. All non-Americans are thrifty.
All Canadians are non-Americans.
All Canadians are thrifty.   (Is it better in this case to symbolize "non-Americans" or "Americans"? Use T,C for the others.)

23. All non-Americans are thrifty.
All Californians are Americans.
All non-Californians are thrifty.   (Can this be reduced to a syllogism? If so use symbols N,T,C.)

24. All non-Americans are thrifty.
All Californians are Americans.
No Californians are thrifty.   (See remarks on No. 23.)

25. All non-Americans dislike orange juice for breakfast.
All Californians like orange juice for breakfast.
All Californians are Americans.   (If this is a syllogism, use symbols A,L,C.)

26. Not all student activities are supported by the college.
Some student activities are supported by the students themselves.
Some things supported by the students themselves are not supported by the college.   (A,C,S)

27. Only a woman would think of unlocking the door with a hairpin.
Only a person who thought of unlocking the door with a hairpin would get in.
Only a woman would get in.   (W,T,G)

28. Cheaters are often discovered.
Those discovered are often punished.
Cheaters are often punished.

29. Englishmen rarely see the point of an American joke.
They rarely laugh when they do.
Englishmen rarely laugh.

30. At least one of my children is in school.
At least one of my children is not in school.
I have at least two children.   (Is this a syllogism? In any case, can its validity or invalidity be established by Venn Diagrams? If so, use symbols C,S.)

SUPPLEMENTARY READINGS

1. Herbert L. Searles, *Logic and Scientific Methods,* New York, The Ronald Press Company, 1958, Ch. 6.

2. Max Black, *Critical Thinking,* New York, Prentice-Hall, Inc., 2d ed., 1952, Ch. 8.

3. Alice Ambrose and Morris Lazerowitz, *Fundamentals of Symbolic Logic,* New York, Rinehart & Company, Inc., 1948, Ch. XI.

15

The Rules for the Syllogism

No syllogism, as we have seen, could be valid if both its premises were particular propositions. Further simple experiments with Venn Diagrams readily establish that the following generalizations also hold.

(a) No valid syllogism could have two negative premises.
(b) No valid syllogism could have one negative premise but an affirmative conclusion.
(c) No valid syllogism could have two affirmative premises but a negative conclusion.
(d) No valid syllogism could have two universal premises but a particular conclusion.
(e) No valid syllogism could have one particular premise but a universal conclusion.

All the statements above are *necessary conditions for validity;* no syllogism could be valid if it ran counter to any one of them. But these statements, as they stand, would not form an entirely satisfactory basis for testing any given syllogism for validity. One difficulty is that they are somewhat redundant; the list above may actually be reduced to a considerable extent without impairing its effectiveness. A more serious defect is that the statements taken together are far from constituting a *sufficient* condition for validity; just because a given syllogism accords with them, it does not follow that it is valid. The syllogism below, for instance, meets all the conditions described above, and yet is still invalid.

(15.1) All dogs are mammals.
       All cats are mammals.
      —————————————
      All cats are dogs.

Thus if we are going to rely on *rules for validity,* we must have more rules than we now have, so as to screen out cases such as 15.1.

In order to state the additional rules in question, it is necessary to introduce at this point one further technical idea. This is the concept of *distribution.* A term appearing in a proposition is said to be *distributed* when the complete verification of the proposition would require a certain grasp of that term not required of other terms. Thus completely to verify "All whales are mammals," one would be obliged either to know all whales, or else to understand the complete meaning of "whale." Thus "whales" is distributed. But "mammals" is not; it is necessary to know only a part of the class of mammals to verify the proposition in question; and a partial familiarity with the *meaning* of this term would also suffice.

Let us try to state this concept more precisely. The *extension* of a term is the class of all objects denoted by that term. The extension of "whale" is all particular whales; that of "red" is all red things. Extension contrasts with *essence;* the *essence* of a term is that group of properties or qualities which belongs commonly and peculiarly to the objects comprising the term's extension. Thus the essence of "whale" might include "aquatic," "mammalian," and "having a horizontal fin," as well as the other properties which as a group are ascribable to *all* whales and *only* to whales. The essence of "red" would involve "next to orange in the spectrum," "having a long wave-length," and so on. Essence and extension will be discussed further in Section 20 (page 218); in that section something will be said about the relations between these concepts and the *definition* of a term.

Returning now to the topic of distribution, we may say that a term is distributed when either its essence or its entire extension must be known in order to verify the proposition in which it occurs, provided that that proposition be factual. Thus the truth of "All whales are mammals" might hinge upon either an enumeration of the extension of "whales" or so complete an understanding of the properties of whales that one could perceive how the possession of these properties would entail that the possessor be a mammal. In case "mammal" were already a part of the essence of "whale," however, the proposition would be logical, and of the form "All S-and-P is P," rather than "All S is P." Our present concern is only with the latter proposition.

In general, S but not P is distributed in an A-proposition. Neither is distributed in an I; to confirm that *some seniors smoke* one would need to know only some seniors and a few of the properties of smoking. Both subject and predicate, on the other hand, are distributed in E; to ascertain that *no* seniors smoke would require precise knowledge of the extension or essence of "senior" as well as of "smoking." Finally, the subject is undistributed but the predicate distributed by O; to verify "Some seniors do not smoke" it is sufficient to be acquainted with only a few seniors, but necessary to know exactly what constitutes smoking. In general, these results are summarized by the rule that *the subject of any universal proposition and the predicate of any negative proposition are distributed.*

The additional rules we need now in order to test any syllogism for validity appear as numbers 4 and 5 below.

1. If both premises are negative, there is no conclusion.
2. If one premise is negative, the conclusion is negative.
3. If both premises are universal, the conclusion is universal.
4. The middle term must be distributed at least once.
5. If a term is distributed in the conclusion, it must be distributed in the premises.

These rules are *necessary and sufficient conditions for validity;* every valid syllogism conforms to them and every syllogism con-

forming to them is valid.   But at present we shall make no attempt
to justify or derive them.   Their complete justification would, in
any event, lie beyond the scope of an elementary course in logic.
In Part Four we shall have something to say about the formal properties of the rules, especially as they exemplify the properties of
sets of postulated laws in general.   The student who feels that
these rules are somewhat arbitrary will in that part at least become familiar with many of their ramifications; perhaps he will
then agree that no other set of laws could surpass these in main-
taining orderly syllogistic argument.   And, in the last analysis,
there could scarcely be any higher criterion for judging logical
rules.

We may, if we like, use these rules immediately to test the validity of particular syllogisms.   Thus 15.1 is invalid because the
middle term "mammals" is undistributed.   And 14.4 (page 138)
fails to be valid because "women" is distributed in the conclusion
but not in the minor premise.   Syllogism 14.1 (page 131) is, on
the other hand, valid; it satisfies all five rules.

But it is possible for us to be much more systematic.   There
are, as has already been pointed out, syllogisms of a great many
different types, depending upon both the arrangement of terms and
the standard forms occurring as premises and conclusion.   A way
of treating these types wholesale would be welcome.

Let us begin by specifying exactly how syllogisms may differ
from each other.   One way is with respect to the arrangement of
terms.   Any one arrangement of terms is called a *figure;* and all
of the figures which syllogisms are capable of assuming reduce to
the four shown below.

M P	P M	M P	P M
S M	S M	M S	M S
S P	S P	S P	S P
1st Figure	*2nd Figure*	*3rd Figure*	*4th Figure*

It is important to remember that in each of these figures, the predicate of the conclusion (*P*) is called the "major term," and the

premise which contains it is referred to as the "major premise." Similarly, the subject of the conclusion (S) is the minor term, and appears also in the minor premise. M, the term eliminated by the premises, is known as the "middle term." This usage with regard to S, P, and M, represents the standard convention for syllogisms, and should be rigorously adhered to. One result of taking this convention seriously is that arrangements of terms which do not appear to belong to any of the figures listed above can be properly classified. For example:

$$X \; Y$$
$$\underline{Y \; Z}$$
$$X \; Z$$

which at first sight seems not to correspond with any of the figures we have named, is not really in the form required by these figures, because its first premise does not contain the predicate of the conclusion. This defect can, however, be remedied by interchanging the premises:

$$Y \; Z$$
$$\underline{X \; Y}$$
$$X \; Z$$

This example clearly shows that the arrangement in question is actually the 1st figure. And simple experimentation along these lines proves that the four figures designated above are really the only ones possible.

Syllogisms also differ with respect to the standard forms assumed by their premises and conclusions. Any one such selection of standard forms is called *mood,* and is identified by designating the forms in the order in which they occur in the syllogism. Thus *AAA* represents a syllogism having an *A*-proposition as its major premise, a second *A*-proposition as its minor premise, and a third *A*-proposition as its conclusion. *IEO* means "that sort of syllogism whose major premise is *I*, whose minor premise is *E*, and whose conclusion is *O*." And similarly for *AII*, *OAO*, *EAE*, and so on. Syllogism 15.1 is of the mood *AAA*. It is, incidentally, in the 2nd figure. The reader would do well to identify the figures and moods of all the syllogisms so far considered.

Since there are four standard forms from which to supply each of the premises and the conclusion of the syllogism, there are $4 \times 4 \times 4$ or 64 possible moods. Since each of these possible moods might occur in any of the four figures, there are 4×64 or 256 possible types of syllogisms. There were, on the other hand, at most seven significant types of conditional argument. This contrast is intended to suggest the value of a wholesale treatment of valid types of the syllogisms.

The problem cannot be solved by supposing that all syllogisms of a certain mood, or of a certain figure, are in general valid. For validity is determined by both mood and figure. *AAA* in the 2nd figure is invalid, as the case of 15.1 shows. But in the 1st figure, *AAA* is valid; an example is

(15.2) All mammals are vertebrates.
          All cats are mammals.
          _____
          All cats are vertebrates.

On the other hand, not every syllogism in the 1st figure is valid. The following illustrates one type that is not:

(15.3) All mammals are vertebrates.
          No snake is a mammal.
          _____
          No snake is a vertebrate.

The task of collecting together all the valid forms of the syllogism is thus more complicated than any analogous problem we have yet had to solve. At best we can only hope to find *which moods are valid in which figures.*

There are, of course, many moods which could not be valid in any figure. *EEE* has two negative premises, and therefore is disqualified by Rule 1. Similarly, *AEA* violates Rule 2, and *AAI* is inconsistent with Rule 3. A great many of the possible moods may without further consideration be ruled out on such grounds.

If we could eliminate all of these invalid moods, we should be left with just those possible moods whose validity depends upon the particular figure in which they are expressed. This would simplify our work considerably.

An apparent drawback, however, is that Rules 1-5, as stated, do not seem to include all of the necessary conditions for validity given at the beginning of this section. *III*, for example, could not possibly be valid in any figure, since it involves two particular premises. Thus we should want to eliminate it at the outset. But none of the rules explicitly adopted appears to make any provision for this case.

The answer is that "If both premises are particular, there is no conclusion" is *implied* by Rules 1-5; it is a *theorem* whose proof we shall shortly state. And this is true for all of the necessary conditions of validity which seem to have been omitted from 1-5. The reader will recall the statement that these conditions, as initially expressed, were somewhat redundant. They are redundant in just the sense that it would be redundant to include among one's assumptions some of the propositions which one wished to prove.

Let us first prove the requisite theorems, and then return to the question "Which moods are valid in each figure?" The first theorem is the one needed to disqualify *III*; it is

Theorem 1. *If both premises are particular, there is no conclusion.*

Proof: Consider every possible case in which both premises are particular. These cases may be symbolized as *II*, *IO*, *OI*, and *OO*. It is easy to see that neither the first nor the last of these combinations could function as the premises of a valid syllogism. If no term is distributed by a single *I*-proposition, then no term is distributed by two *I*-propositions; hence the middle term would be undistributed by the combination *II*. But this violates Rule 4. And *OO*, having both premises negative violates Rule 1 outright.

Subtler reasoning is required to establish that any syllogism having *IO* or *OI* as its premises would be invalid. In the first place, the conclusion must, by Rule 2, be negative in either case. This means that the major term must be distributed in the conclusion and hence in the major premise. Since exactly one term is distributed by either *OI* or *IO*, this conclusion is so far feasible. But by Rule 4, the middle term must also be distributed. Because the one term distributed by *OI* or *IO* is the major term, which has already been pre-empted, this last requirement cannot be met, and the syllogism is invalid. This completes the proof of Theorem 1.

Next we shall demonstrate

Theorem 2: *If one premise is particular, the conclusion is particular.*

Proof: Let us consider the combinations of premises available when one premise is particular. By Theorem 1 we know that when one is particular, the other must be universal if there is to be any conclusion at all. Thus the possible combinations are *IA, AI, IE, EI, OA, AO, OE,* and *EO.* The last two are immediately eliminated by Rule 1. *IE* must also be stricken from the list because, having a negative conclusion, its major term must be distributed in the conclusion but cannot be distributed in the affirmative particular major premise. Five possibilities, however, remain; let us classify them as affirmative or negative, and show that in either case the conclusion must be particular.

The combinations leading to an affirmative conclusion are *IA* and *AI.* In such a syllogism only the subject of the *A*-proposition could be distributed in the premises; this must therefore be the middle term. So no distributed term is left over for the conclusion. Thus the conclusion must be *I,* and so particular. The remaining combinations are *EI, OA,* and *AO.* In each case, just two terms are distributed in the premises. One of these must be the middle term and the other the major term. But if the conclusion were universal, the minor term would also have to be distributed. Since this is impossible, the conclusion must be particular. Therefore, Theorem 2 is established in general.

Finally, we need to prove a theorem which corresponds with statement (c) of the list of criteria given at the beginning of this section.

Theorem 3. *If both premises are affirmative, the conclusion must be affirmative.*

Proof: Let us assume the contradictory of what we wish to prove, and show that this assumption has absurd consequences. This procedure is a further concrete illustration of *indirect proof* (see Section 8, page 56). The contradictory of "If both premises are affirmative, the conclusion must be affirmative" is "Both premises are affirmative, but the conclusion is negative." Assuming this, we note that the major term will have to be distributed in the conclusion, since it is the predicate of a negative proposition. In this case the major term must be distributed in the major premise, by Rule 5. Now the assumption is that both premises are affirmative; this means that neither may have a distributed predicate. Thus the major term must be the subject of the major premise. So far, we can sketch in the following necessary outlines of an argument assumed to have two affirmative premises but a negative conclusion:

$$P \ * \quad (P \text{ distributed})$$
$$* \ *$$
$$\overline{S \ P}$$

The rest follows easily. The major premise must be universal, having a distributed subject; since it is affirmative, it must, in fact, be *A*. Now the predicate of the major premise must, of course, be *M*, and since *M* is undistributed here, it must, by Rule 4, be distributed in the minor premise. This can be the case only if *M* is the subject of the minor premise; since again a premise with a distributed *predicate*, being negative, would fail to meet the terms of our assumption. Thus the minor premise must be "*MS*," and have the form of an *A*-proposition. Since *S* is undistributed here it cannot, by Rule 5, be distributed in the conclusion. Therefore, the conclusion is *O*; and the argument as a whole must read

All *P* is *M*
All *M* is *S*
Some *S* is not *P*

This is *AAO* in the 4th Figure. But by Rule 3, this syllogism, having two universal premises and a particular conclusion, is invalid. Hence no syllogism may have two affirmative premises and a negative conclusion. And this is what we had set out to prove.

These five rules and three theorems regarding the validity of syllogistic arguments are now immediately applicable to the problem of ascertaining in detail which of the possible syllogisms are valid. Of the possible combinations of premises, for example, Rule 1 eliminates the quarter comprising two negative premises, and Theorem 1 debars almost another quarter of the possibilities. Rules 2 and 3 and Theorems 2 and 3 enable us to decide precisely what conclusion is required by each of the combinations still eligible. At this stage, the only moods of the syllogism which could possibly be valid in any figure of the syllogism are the following:

(1) *AAA*	(4) *AEE*	(7) *OAO*
(2) *AII*	(5) *EAE*	(8) *IAI*
(3) *AOO*	(6) *EIO*	(9) *IEO*

But the last of these must be eliminated in accordance with an observation made in connection with the proof of Theorem 2: namely, the *I* major premise does not distribute the major term, but the *O* conclusion does. Only eight moods, then, are left. But not all eight are valid in each figure; *AAA,* as we already know, is invalid in the 2nd figure. To determine the moods valid in each figure, we need only note the manner in which each of (1) through (8) above distributes its terms as they are differently arranged by each figure.

Consider, for example, *AAA* in the 1st figure. Here *M* is distributed and *P* undistributed in the minor premise, and *S* is distributed while *P* is undistributed in the conclusion. Since this is in perfect conformity with the rules, we may conclude that this argument is generally valid. *AAA* in the 2nd figure, on the other hand, is invalid; for *M* is undistributed in both the major premise and the minor premise.

Thus each of the eight possible moods may be tested in each of the four figures. But this work can be greatly facilitated through the use of certain theorems which apply to particular figures. These Theorems can be exemplified by two which together are necessary and sufficient for validity in the 1st figure.

Theorem 4: *In the 1st figure, the minor premise must be affirmative.*

Proof: In the 1st figure, the arrangement of terms is

$$M\ P$$
$$S\ M$$
$$\overline{S\ P}$$

Let us assume that the minor premise is negative, and show that this leads to an absurdity; as in the case of Theorem 3, we are thus making use of indirect proof. Now if the minor premise is negative, the conclusion must be negative, by Rule 2. And if the conclusion is negative, the major term P must be distributed in the conclusion. But if P is distributed in the conclusion, Rule 5 requires it to be distributed in the major premise. This makes the major premise negative since any proposition with a distributed predicate is negative. Thus there are two negative premises. But this violates Rule 1. Therefore, the minor premise cannot be negative. It must be affirmative.

Theorem 5: *In the 1st figure, the major premise must be universal.*

Proof: We may proceed directly here; we do not need to use indirect proof. According to Theorem 4, the minor premise is affirmative. This means that the middle term M is undistributed in this premise. By Rule 5, it must, however, be distributed once, and so it must be distributed in the major premise. But this means that the major premise has a distributed subject, and therefore is universal. This is what we wanted to prove.

Knowing these two facts about the 1st figure, we have only to inspect the list of possible moods given above in order to see which of them are valid in this figure, that is, which of the moods involve a universal major premise and an affirmative minor premise. Only four of the possible moods qualify, namely, *AAA, AII, EAE,* and *EIO.*

The application of this procedure to the other three figures will be the basis of one of the exercises to follow this section. All in all, just fifteen moods are valid in one or another of the figures. This statement is, however, true only on the assumption that universal propositions are interpreted hypothetically. If we had adopted the existential interpretation, we should have to test the possible moods for validity on the basis of a somewhat different set of rules. In that case, twenty-four types of syllogism would be valid. *AAI, AEO,* and *EAO* would represent added possibilities, since there would now be no reason to exclude those moods involving two universal premises and a particular conclusion.

In this section, we have been discussing the syllogism from a rather abstract point of view. This abstractness is motivated at least partly by the desire to anticipate the study of systematic order which will concern us in Part Four. But it is well to note how the present section differs from our treatment of earlier topics. Instead of merely showing how specific arguments might be tested for validity, we have laid the groundwork here for an exhaustive list of valid forms. We should not on this account, however, ignore the consideration that the rules given above may be used directly as tests of validity. One need consult no catalogue of valid forms, for instance, to see that example 15.1, given at the beginning of this section, is invalid by virtue of having an undistributed middle term.

Such violations of Rule 4 are among the most common fallacious syllogisms; and the error in question is usually identified simply as the *fallacy of undistributed middle.* Other common fallacies are those which violate Rule 5; a case in point is

(15.4) All pines are coniferous
        No pines are oaks
        _____
        No oaks are coniferous,

in which the major term "coniferous" is distributed in the conclusion but not in the major premise. This fallacy is known as *illicit process of the major.* Similarly, there is a fallacy of illicit process of the minor.

A syllogism is necessarily restricted to three terms, and any argument which seems to be a syllogism but actually contains four terms will be fallacious. For no "middle term" can then be justifiably eliminated. This *fallacy of four terms* may be illustrated as follows:

(15.5) Whatever goes up must come down.
      Prices have gone up.
      ———————————————————
      Prices will come down.

Here there is an ambiguity in the term "thing that goes up," which in the major premise refers to a physical object acting within a gravitational field, but in the minor premise has a completely different meaning.

Two special cases of the fallacy of four terms are the fallacies of *composition* and *division,* in which the properties of individuals are confused with those of classes. An example is

(15.6) Metals are abundant.
      Gold is a metal.
      ———————————————————
      Gold is abundant.

In 15.6 the word "metals" in the major premise refers to the *class* of all metals; *as a class,* metals frequently occur. But the "metal" in the minor premise represents only an individual member of the class. As a result, the conclusion attributes a property of the class as a whole to an individual member of the class. This syllogism exemplifies the fallacy of *division.* The fallacy of *composition,* on the other hand, occurs when inattention to the middle term permits the attribution of a property of individuals to the class as a whole of which the individuals are members. For instance,

(15.7) Every event has a cause.
      Nature is every event.
      ———————————————————
      Nature has a cause.

Both the fallacy of composition and that of division can be described as a confusion between the *collective* and the *distributive* use of the middle term. Any term is used *distributively* when a certain property is ascribed to each member of the class it denotes. Thus "Metals are lustrous" involves the distributive use of "metals," since it ascribes luster to each and every individual member of the class of metals.   A term is used *collectively,* on the other hand, when a property is ascribed to the class as a whole which is denoted by the term, as in "Metals are abundant."   The fallacy of division occurs when the middle term is used collectively in the major premise and distributively in the minor; the fallacy of composition involves a middle term which is distributive in the major premise but collective in the minor.   Actually, terms used collectively should be avoided altogether in syllogisms and other arguments depending upon the traditional analysis of propositions. Where a term is used collectively *twice,* the error is even more obvious, as in

(15.8)   Metals are abundant.
        Gold is not abundant.

        Gold is not a metal.

In sum, the theory of syllogisms is not only a simple and readily comprehensible illustration of systematic order, but also an effective criterion for judging arguments.   Yet it is subject to certain severe limitations.   To explore these is one of the purposes of the succeeding section.

EXERCISES

A. Indicate which terms are distributed in each proposition occurring in Exercise D of Section 12 (pages 111-12).

B. (a) Use the rules discussed in the present section to test each syllogism in the exercise following Section 14 (pages 139-41). (b) Identify the figure and mood of each of these syllogisms.

C. What fallacies, if any, occur in each of the following syllogisms?

    1. Great works of art carry a universal message.
       The symphonies of Haydn are great works of art.

       The symphonies of Haydn carry a universal message.

2. Great works of art are rare.
   The symphonies of Haydn are great works of art.

   ___
   The symphonies of Haydn are rare.
3. Great works of art are never merely autobiographical.
   Great works of art always carry a universal message.

   ___
   Nothing which is merely autobiographical carries a universal message.
4. All criminal actions are punishable by law.
   Felony is a criminal action.

   ___
   Felony is punishable by law.
5. All criminal actions are punishable by law.
   A trial for felony is a criminal action.

   ___
   A trial for felony is punishable by law.
6. All criminal actions are punishable by law.
   Some civil actions are not criminal actions.

   ___
   Some civil actions are not punishable by law.
7. All the King's horses and all the King's men could not put Humpty together again.
   All the King's horses and all the King's men were an army.

   ___
   No army could put Humpty together again.
8. Tea-tasters are wage-earners.
   Wage-earners are not scarce.

   ___
   Tea-tasters are not scarce.
9. All tea-tasters are wage-earners.
   The Tea Society consists of all tea-tasters.

   ___
   The Tea Society consists of all wage-earners.
10. Some silicosis is dangerous.
    All silicosis is rare.

    ___
    Some rare things are dangerous.

D. On the basis of the five rules given in this section, prove each of the following theorems.

1. In the 2nd figure, the conclusion must be negative.
   (*Hint:* Assume that the conclusion is *affirmative,* and proceed by indirect proof. If the conclusion is affirmative, can either premise be negative? What then?)
2. In the 2nd figure, the major premise must be universal.
   (*Hint:* See whether this is directly implied by No. 1, above.)
3. In the 3rd figure, the minor premise must be affirmative.

    (*Hint:* Use indirect proof. If the minor premise is *negative,* what follows? What contradiction is ultimately reached?)

    4. In the 3rd figure, the conclusion must be particular.

       (*Hint:* See whether this is directly implied by No. 3, above.)

    5. In the 4th figure, if the conclusion is negative, the major premise is universal.

    6. In the 4th figure, if the major premise is affirmative, the minor premise is universal.

    7. In the 4th figure, if the minor premise is affirmative, the conclusion is particular.

    8. Prove that in general if the minor term is the predicate of the minor premise, the conclusion cannot be *A.*

    9. Prove that in general if the major term is the predicate of the major premise, the minor premise must be affirmative.

    10. Prove that *EIO* is valid in every figure. (Do not consult particular figures.)

E. On the basis of the conclusions you have just reached in Exercise D, above, and the theorems for the 1st figure proven in the text of this section, make an exhaustive list of the moods of the syllogism valid in each figure.

F. Solve each of the following problems without consulting the results of Exercise E.

    1. What one valid syllogism has an *A* conclusion?

    2. What one valid syllogism has an *O* major premise?

    3. What one valid syllogism has an *O* minor premise?

    4. A certain valid syllogism has a major premise of *I,* and the major term is the subject of the major premise. What is it?

    5. What one valid syllogism, whose middle term is undistributed in the major premise and is the predicate of the minor premise, has an *E* conclusion?

SUPPLEMENTARY READINGS

1. J. N. Keynes, *Studies and Exercises in Formal Logic,* London, Macmillan and Co., 1906, Pt. III, Ch. I.

2. Morris R. Cohen and Ernest Nagel, *An Introduction to Logic and Scientific Method,* New York, Harcourt, Brace and Company, Inc., 1934, Bk. I, Ch. IV.

3. Ralph M. Eaton, *General Logic*, New York, Charles Scribner's Sons, 1931, Pt. II, Ch. IX.

4. W. Stanley Jevons, *Elementary Lessons in Logic*, London, Macmillan and Co., 1893, Lessons XIV-XIX.

16

Relations

Many arguments frequently occurring in inquiry and discourse cannot be criticized by syllogistic rules even though they seem to have exactly the form of syllogisms. One troublesome case is the following:

(16.1) Five is greater than two.
Seven is greater than five.

Seven is greater than two.

The illusion that 16.1 is a syllogism breaks down when we attempt to isolate its terms. Perhaps the simplest rendering of 16.1 in subject–predicate form is

(16.2) Five is a number greater than two.
Seven is a number greater than five.

Seven is a number greater than two.

This paraphrase has the virtue of exhibiting a subject and a predicate joined by a copulative verb as the structure of each of its premises and conclusion. However, 16.2 as it stands is not a syllogism, since it involves four terms; there is no clear-cut middle term at all. To correct this defect, we may seek to express 16.2 as

(16.3) Any number greater than five is a number greater than two.
Seven is a number greater than five.

Seven is a number greater than two.

160

But 16.3 serves only to reveal the impossibility of expressing the argument in question in syllogistic form at all. For while we now have a syllogism, we have lost the original argument. The major premise of 16.3 concerns numbers *greater than* five, while the initial assumption of 16.1 had to do with five itself. And, in general, no amount of "tinkering" can make the two arguments equivalent.

Other arguments commonly employed are even more obviously incapable of being tested by any technique developed so far in this book. The following are examples:

(16.4) Philadelphia is east of Pittsburgh.
Scranton is north of Philadelphia.
———————————————————
Scranton is northeast of Pittsburgh.

(16.5) The drugstore is between the theater and the grocery store.
The theater is to the right of the drugstore.
———————————————————
The drugstore is to the right of the grocery store.

(16.6) Boggs's stepdaughter is married to Boggs's father.
Anyone married to Boggs's father is Boggs's mother.
The father of Boggs's mother is Boggs's grandfather.
———————————————————
Boggs is his own grandfather.

(16.7) Boggs is the teacher of Diggs.
Diggs is a nephew of Meggs.
———————————————————
Meggs is the uncle of a student of Boggs.

The fruitful analysis of arguments like 16.1 and 16.4-16.7 depends upon the insight that more than just subject and predicate are involved in most of the propositions comprising these arguments. What is also peculiarly significant is the way in which the terms of each proposition are related to each other. The relationship is generally more explicit and more complex than the connection expressed by a simple copulative verb. It has already been indicated, for instance, what perplexities confront the effort to express a simple arithmetical inequality in terms of a copula. It is only when we take seriously the idea expressed by "is greater than" that we properly understand such a proposition. "Is greater than" is thus an essential constant. Other such constants, occurring in

16.4 through 16.7, are "is east of," "is north of," "is northeast of," "is between," "is to the right of," "is married to," "is the father of," "is the teacher of," and so on. Let us call such constants *relations*. Since the idea of a relation is fully as general as that of logic itself, it would be futile to attempt to define it in terms of any concept with which the reader is likely to be better acquainted. At best, we can only make the rather circular stipulation that a relation is whatever relates terms.

The theory of relations differs from most of the material presented so far in that the precise technique for criticizing relational arguments lies beyond the scope of this book. All that we can do here is to state some of the considerations which would govern the development of any such theory. A statement of these considerations may at least result in the student's gaining a heightened sense of the significance of relations.

One important goal of a theory of relations would be generality. It should by now be clear that complete generality is indeed characteristic of logic as a whole; for when the criticism of any argument depends on the knowledge of any specific detail or fact, that criticism is not logical. Thus if the theory of relations is to belong to logic rather than to any narrower discipline, it must be independent of any particular assumption made in science or common sense. Examples would be the assumptions of arithmetic, geometry, cartography, and genealogy. To speak more directly, if 16.1 is valid, then its logical truth is not merely a truth of arithmetic; 16.1 must rather exhibit a form holding for all disciplines. Similarly the validity of 16.4 must be purely formal, and may depend upon no properties peculiar to map directions. And 16.5 and 16.6 must also exhibit structures independent of any particular relational content.

Our fundamental concern, then, is with the wholly general properties of relations. Among these properties is that of requiring a specific number of terms. Two terms, for example, are necessary to make a complete proposition of "is east of"; for this is not a proposition in itself, nor is the expression, "Philadelphia is east of." Similarly, "greater than," "is to the right of," and "is the father of" possess the common property of relating just two terms. We shall call such relations *dyadic*. Not all relations are dyadic; as 16.5 indicates, "between" takes three terms, and is accordingly classified as *triadic*. A *tetradic* relation would be the usage of "buys" involved in *"Boggs* buys *an automobile* from *Diggs* for *two thousand dollars."*

By this scheme of nomenclature, any relation capable of taking only *one* term would be *monadic*. But this description precisely fits a *class*. Classes are thus monadic relations. To illustrate the continuity of classes with relations taking more than one term, we may write the series

(16.8) Boggs is male.
(16.9) Boggs is the father-in-law of Diggs.
(16.10) Boggs recommended Diggs to Meggs.
(16.11) Boggs and Diggs played bridge against Meggs and Suggs.

This series of relational propositions does not constitute a *proof* of anything, but it does show that the function of a class, such as "male" in 16.8, is similar to that of the relations involved in 16.9, 16.10, and 16.11. The only difference is one of simplicity; because it contains one noun, 16.8 is simpler than 16.9, which contains two, or 16.10, which involves three. Thus if "is the father-in-law of" is a two-termed relation, and "recommended . . . to . . ." is three-termed, it is consistent to regard "male" as one-termed, or monadic.

Monadic relations, at least under the guise of classes, have already been discussed at some length in connection with the traditional analysis of propositions into subject and predicate. The tendency of the more modern approach to propositions, on the other hand, would be to emphasize relations of higher degree than monadic. Instead of treating "Whales are mammals," for instance, as primarily a case of subject and predicate, it would focus on the dyadic relation "are." One would note, perhaps, that the "are" in "Whales are mammals" is not at all like the "are" in

"Whales are scarce," since *mammal* is a property of each whale individually, whereas *scarce* characterizes only the class of all whales. Thus the "are" must relate the predicate to the subject differently in each of these cases. So it becomes important to elaborate the properties of relations other than monadic. In particular, dyadic relations may be classified according to certain wholly general properties. And such a classification is useful in explaining the various ways in which "are" behaves, as well as much else of significance.

One of the properties by which we may classify relations is *symmetry*. A relation is symmetrical when, from the assumption that it holds between *a* and *b*, one is justified in inferring that the same relation holds between *b* and *a*. Thus "equals" is symmetrical; for if *a* equals *b,* then *b* equals *a*. Another symmetrical relation is "is a classmate of"; Boggs is a classmate of Diggs if, and only if, Diggs is a classmate of Boggs. But "is greater than" is not symmetrical; indeed from the fact that *a* is greater than *b*, it may be inferred that *b* is *not* greater than *a*. Any relation which, like "is greater than," can hold only in one direction, is called *asymmetrical*. Other examples of asymmetrical relations are "is to the right of," "is the father of," and "defeats."

If a symmetrical relation always holds in both directions, and an asymmetrical one holds in one direction only, then these two properties are not logically exhaustive; for there remains the possibility that a relation might hold sometimes in one direction and at other times in both. Thus if Boggs hates Diggs, it by no means follows that Diggs hates Boggs. And "George is the brother of Lee" should not be thought to involve a symmetrical relation, for the simple reason that Lee might be female. Relations like "hates" and "is the brother of" are classified as *nonsymmetrical*.

The copulative verb may be variously symmetrical, nonsymmetrical, or asymmetrical, depending upon the context in which it occurs. "Is" or "are" is symmetrical when it means "equals" or "is identical with" as it does in "Two plus two is four." The copula acts as a nonsymmetrical relation when it ascribes a property to the individual members of a class; "Whales are mammals" does not logically imply the falsity of "Mammals are whales." But the "are" in "Whales are scarce" is, for obvious reasons, asymmetrical.

A classification which cuts across that just given may be made with respect to *transitivity*. In general, a relation is *transitive* when, if it holds between *a* and *b*, and also between *b* and *c*, one may infer that it holds between *a* and *c*. "Is greater than" is transitive, for if *a* is greater than *b* and *b* is greater than *c*, then *a* is greater than *c*. So is "is an ancestor of." But "is a parent of" is *intransitive;* if George I is a parent of George II, and the latter is a parent of George III, then we may be assured that George I is *not* a parent of George III. Many relations are neither transitive nor intransitive, but instead are *nontransitive.* Thus if Boggs is a friend of Diggs, and Diggs a friend of Meggs, then Boggs may or may not be a friend of Meggs.

If we are to argue syllogistically, the copulative verb must be transitive; from "*a* is *b* and *b* is *c*" we want a clear title to conclude, as in *AAA* of the 1st figure, that *a* is *c*. But "is" and "are" are not always transitive. Just because gold is a metal and metals are abundant, it does not follow that gold is abundant. The fallacies of composition and division are both traceable to the erroneous assumption that the copula which ascribes some property to a class as a whole is transitive.

One general result of a detailed examination of the copulative verb is that the entire theory of the syllogism becomes a special case of the study of relations. Other special cases are the arguments 16.1 and 16.4-16.7, the criteria of whose validity are expressible in terms of symmetry, transitivity, and other such general properties. But it has already been indicated that such criteria lie beyond the scope of this text.

We shall not, however, permit the present section to end on this pessimistic note. For there are symbolic calculations with respect to relations which are well within the competence of the elementary student. A certain type of problem, for example, may be solved in terms of symbols for the *converse* of a relation, and for the *relative product* of any two relations.

Whenever a thing bears any relation to another, we may express this idea as aRb, where a and b are the things related and R is the relation.   Thus aRb might mean "Boggs sits next to Suggs," "saccharin is sweeter than sugar," or "2 is the square root of 4," depending upon the particular values of a, b, and R.   Now the *converse* of R, written R', is the relation b bears to a when aRb is true.   Thus the converse of "is sweeter than" is "is not as sweet as," and the converse of "is the square root of" is "is the square of"; sugar is not as sweet as saccharin and 4 is the square of 2. The converse of "sits next to" is that relation itself, and generally a symmetrical relation is its own converse.

The *relative product* of two relations, say R and S, is the complex relation between a and b when a bears R to something which in turn bears S to b.   It is symbolized R/S.   Suppose that R means "sits next to," and S means "is a friend of."   Then aR/Sb means "a sits next to a friend of b."   On this scheme, aS/Rb would mean "a is a friend of whoever sits next to b."   One thing that we have succeeded in showing is that R/S is not generally equivalent to S/R.   For the person who sits next to a friend of b is not necessarily a friend of the person who sits next to b.

The problem which we are now in a position to solve is that of defining all the relationships in a family tree in terms of only one of these relationships.   Let us single out the relation "is a child of" as the point of departure.   Call it C.   Then, since "is a parent of" is the converse of "is a child of," we may write

(16.12)   "Is a parent of" $= C'$.

A grandparent of is a parent of a parent of, so

(16.13)   "Is a grandparent of" $= C'/C'$.

On the other hand,

(16.14)   "Is a grandchild of" $= C/C$.

To express the idea that *a* is the sibling (brother or sister) of *b*, we need only reflect that *a* and *b* are siblings when they are children of the same parent. Thus

(16.15) "Is a sibling of" = C/C'.

To define "sibling" exactly, of course, we should have to take account of the possibility that *a* and *b* might be the same person; for *a* is the child of his own parent, yet not his own sibling. We should also need to specify that *a* and *b* have the same mother *and* father. But these technical details may, for our limited purposes, be overlooked.

Suppose now that we wish to define "is a cousin of." If *a* is a cousin of *b*, then *a* is a child of an uncle or aunt of *b*. But an uncle or aunt is a sibling of a parent.

(16.16) "Is an uncle or aunt of" = $(C/C')/C'$.

Thus

(16.17) "Is a cousin of" = $C/[(C/C')/C']$.

An interesting point, however, is that the parentheses are actually irrelevant to 16.17; they may be removed, and the relations themselves may be grouped in any way we choose (provided we read them in the same order), without distorting the meaning of "cousin." For example,

(16.18) "Is a cousin of" = $(C/C)/(C'/C')$,

since a cousin is a grandchild of a grandparent. Of course, the qualifications noted in connection with 16.15 would still have to be assumed.

EXERCISES

A. Which of the following arguments are incapable of being tested for validity by means of the techniques discussed prior to the present section? Where you *can* test them, do so.

1. Whatever travels faster than a train must make the trip from New York to Boston in less than five hours.
An airplane travels faster than a train.
___
An airplane must make the trip from New York to Boston in less than five hours.

2. An airplane travels faster than a train.
A train travels faster than a bus.
___
An airplane travels faster than a bus.

3. If an airplane travels faster than a train, then an airplane travels faster than a bus.
If an airplane travels faster than a bus, then an airplane travels faster than a bicycle.
___
If an airplane travels faster than a train, then an airplane travels faster than a bicycle.

4. All of my aunts are married.
___
None of my aunts is unmarried.

5. All of my aunts are sisters of my mother.
___
All of my aunts have the same father.

6. No one who is the sister of my mother is the sister of my father.
All of my aunts are sisters of my mother.
___
None of my aunts is the sister of my father.

7. If Boggs lives next door to Meggs, then Boggs does not often telephone Meggs. But Boggs does telephone Meggs quite often. Therefore, Boggs does not live next door to Meggs.

8. If Boggs lives next door to Meggs, and Meggs lives next door to Diggs, then Boggs does not live next door to Diggs.

9. Boggs lives next door to Meggs. Therefore, Meggs lives next door to Boggs.

10. If Boggs lives next door to Meggs, then Boggs lives on the west side of the town. Therefore, if Boggs does not live on the west side of the town, he does not live next door to Meggs.

B. Classify each of the following dyadic relations. (Symmetrical, nonsymmetrical, or asymmetrical? Transitive, nontransitive, or intransitive?)

1. Travels faster than
2. Is the sister of
3. Lives next door to
4. Marries

5. Marries for money
6. Is as wealthy as
7. Is wealthier than
8. Is $1,000 wealthier than
9. Is included in
10. Is excluded from
11. Has defeated
12. Has tied with
13. Puts both arms around
14. Implies
15. Is the obverse of
16. Is the converse of
17. Is the contradictory of
18. *Is*, as in "The sum of two and two is four"
19. *Are*, as in "Accidents are dangerous"
20. *Are*, as in "Accidents are frequent"

C. Show by means of examples that each of the following propositions is false. But use examples other than those occurring in the present section, in your class discussion, or in Exercise B, above.

1. If a relation is symmetrical, it must be transitive.
2. If a relation is asymmetrical, it must be transitive.
3. If a relation is nonsymmetrical, it must be transitive.
4. If a relation is transitive, it must be symmetrical.
5. If a relation is intransitive, it must be symmetrical.
6. If a relation is nontransitive, it must be symmetrical.
7. If a relation is nontransitive, it must be asymmetrical.
8. If a relation is nontransitive, it must be nonsymmetrical.
9. If a relation is nonsymmetrical, it must be nontransitive.
10. If a relation is asymmetrical, it must be intransitive.

D. Football forecasters distinguish between the theoretical relation *is stronger than* (as in "Team A is stronger than Team B," often made more explicit by adding the qualification "on paper") and the nontheoretical relation "has defeated." The former of these relations may be symbolized S, and the latter D.

(a) Using these symbols, as well as the symbols for the converse of a relation and for the relative product of two relations, express each of the following statements. Consider that *a* and *b* are football teams.

1. *a* is weaker than *b*.
2. *a* has lost to *b*.
3. *a* has lost to a team which has lost to *b*.
4. *a* has lost to a team which is stronger than *b*.
5. *a* is stronger than a team which has lost to *b*.
6. *a* has defeated a team which is stronger than *b*.
7. *a* is stronger than a team which is stronger than *b*.
8. *a* has defeated a team which has defeated *b*.
9. *a* is weaker than a team which is stronger than *b*.
10. *a* is stronger than a team which is weaker than *b*.

(b) Which, if any, of statements 3-10 *necessarily* implies a factual conclusion? What conclusion?

(c) Do statements 4 and 5 mean the same? Do 9 and 10?

(d) 1. Does $aD'b$ mean $-(aDb)$? Explain.
    2. Does $aS'b$ mean $-(aSb)$? Explain.
    3. Does $aS'/S'b$ imply $aS'b$? Explain.
    4. Does $aD'/D'b$ imply $aD'b$? Explain.
    5. Does aSb imply $bS'a$? Explain.

SUPPLEMENTARY READINGS

1. Alfred Tarski, *Introduction to Logic and to the Methodology of Deductive Sciences,* New York, Oxford University Press, 1941, Ch. V.

2. Morris R. Cohen and Ernest Nagel, *An Introduction to Logic and Scientific Method,* New York, Harcourt, Brace and Company, Inc., 1934, Ch. VI, Sec. 2.

17

Some Elementary Aspects
of Quantification

Sections 12-15 constitute a survey of the traditional approach to the logic of classes. But there is also a more modern approach, some of the motives for which are suggested by Section 16. The present section is an attempt to indicate further ramifications of present-day logical analysis, in the hope of showing its capacity to deal with problems far more complicated than those that traditional logic undertook to solve.

In contemporary logic, classes, or monadic relations, are often symbolized by the capital letters F, G, and H, and their terms, or members, are denoted by x, y, and z, written to the right of the symbols for the respective classes to which they belong. Thus Fx means "x is a member of the class F," and Gy signifies that y belongs to the class G or, if one will, that y has the *property G*. All these letters are *variables;* they represent inessential components of logical structures. Suppose, for instance, that the phrase "the book is red" occurred in a logically true proposition in such a way that "book" and "red" were both inessential to the truth of this proposition. In such a case, we should replace "the book is red" by a combination such as Fx.

Now it is the occurrence in a logical truth of a word, such as "all," "some," or "none," which expresses quantity, that, in particular, gives this sort of analysis its peculiar justification. For when such a word occurs, no technique of the propositional calculus is capable of ascertaining the truth-value of the proposition as a whole. The following proposition illustrates the efficacy of using symbols for inessential classes and their inessential members.

(17.1) Either all books are red or some books are not red.

This is a logical truth to which the class "red" and the members "books" are alike inessential. Let us rephrase it in terms of the new variables which recognize the distinction between a class and its members. "All books are red" means "Whatever books there are, they are red"; and "Some books are not red" means "There are some books such that they are not red." This apparently trivial transformation enables us to express the logical structure of 17.1 as

(17.2) (Whatever x's there are, Fx) v (there are some x's such that -Fx)

Now no method hitherto developed in this book is capable of testing the truth of 17.2. Truth-tables fail to apply to it because the propositional calculus can perceive neither the inner structuration of the two alternated components of 17.2, nor the subtle relation between these components; a truth-table for 17.2 would necessarily be a truth-table for "p v q," which is not logically true. The rules of the syllogism are likewise ineffectual, for 17.2 is not a syllogism. It is rather a logical truth of a new sort, and one which can be adequately expressed only in terms of the symbols which are now advocated.

Two more symbols will complete the vocabulary necessary for this section. These are notations for the essential phrases, "Whatever x's there are," and "there are some x's such that." To represent the former phrase, we shall enclose x in parentheses, so that "Whatever x's there are" becomes simply (x). To indicate the latter, we shall write simply (Ex). These particular symbols, or *quantifiers,* stand always to the left of the expressions which they quantify. The following propositions represent the proper use of quantifiers:

(17.3) (x) Fx
(17.4) (Ex) Fx
(17.5) (x) $-Fx$
(17.6) $-[(x)$ $Fx]$
(17.7) (Ex) $(Fx$ & $Gx)$
(17.8) (x) $(Fx \rightarrow Gx)$
(17.9) (x) Fx v (Ex) $-Fx$

Let us read these off. Proposition 17.3 means, "Whatever x there is, x is F," or more idiomatically, "All x is F." Other versions are "Every x is F," "Any x is F," "Each x is F," and "Any x you choose is F." "Everything is F" would also be a correct rendition. Quantification by (x) is known as *universal quantification,* because through it the class quantified is alleged to be a property of the universe as a whole. If everything were red, then redness would be such a property.

The opposite of universal quantification is *existential quantification,* and this occurs in 17.4. (Ex) Fx alleges that at least one thing exists belonging to the class F. It may be read "There are some x's such that Fx," or "Some x's are F," or "At least one x is F," or "Something is F."

Proposition 17.5 means literally, "Whatever x there is, x is not F"; which is to say, no x is F. The meaning of 17.5 must not be confused with that of 17.6, which alleges only that it is false that all x is F. If 17.5 is true, so is 17.6; but the converse of this by no means follows. According to 17.7, at least one thing is both F and G; for example, at least one object in the world is both red and square. What 17.8 alleges is that whatever x one may choose, if x is F, then it is G. An instance of this would be "Whatever x you choose, if x is human then x is mortal." This form, consisting of a universal quantifier operating over a conditional, is the structure of the A-proposition in the theory of the syllogism, whenever this proposition is assumed to have no existential import; it is also the structure of any scientific law.   Finally, 17.9 represents in more compact form the logical truth which 17.2, above, expresses.

Quantification theory is the general theory through which arguments involving quantifiers may be tested for validity.   Expediency in outlining the scope of this theory will result if we first point out that the universal quantifier and the existential quantifier are not independent; they are, in fact, mutually definable.   For all that "Everything is *F*" alleges is, "It is false that there is something which is not *F*"; in other words,

(17.10) (*x*) *Fx* means -(*Ex*) -*Fx*

Similarly "Something is *F*" is equivalent with "It is not the case that everything is not *F*"; or

(17.11) (*Ex*) *Fx* means -(*x*) -*Fx*

Whatever is unfamiliar about 17.10 and 17.11 can best be understood through thoughtful consideration of examples that may come to mind.   What does it mean, for instance, to say, as the materialist does, "Everything is a material object"?   Is not this simply the contradictory of the nonmaterialistic assertion "At least one thing is not a material object"?

Another way of expressing the relationship between a universal quantifier and an existential quantifier involves denying both sides of 17.10 and 17.11, respectively.   As a result, we have

(17.12) -(*x*) *Fx* ←→ - -(*Ex*) -*Fx*, or -(*x*) *Fx* ←→ (*Ex*) -*Fx*
(17.13) -(*Ex*) *Fx* ←→ - -(*x* -*Fx*, or -(*Ex*) *Fx* ←→ (*x*) -*Fx*

These reformulations elucidate an important aspect of human controversy: A universally quantified proposition may be refuted through the display of one contrary instance, but in order to overthrow an existentially quantified proposition, one must produce a general statement or law.   Thus it is much safer to assert that a thing exists than that it does not; and anyone who asserts a generalization takes an indefinitely large risk of being contradicted by a single instance. Yet the taking of such risks is an imperative of human knowledge, which progresses only as it brings isolated facts together under general laws. Much of the difference between medieval and modern science can be explained by the fact that the former took the easy course of asserting unrelated existentially quantified propositions, while the latter took enormous risks in committing itself to universal statements. And principally because it took these risks, modern science has had remarkable success. For example, the medieval biologist believed that there were animals having the body and legs of a lion and the wings and beak of an eagle; these he called "griffins." Nothing but imagination is required to assert "(Ex) x is a griffin"; but the courage of a fundamental conviction is involved in its denial by the modern biologist. His assertion, "(x) -$(x$ is a griffin$)$" requires courage because the discovery of a single griffin on this planet would confute his entire theory of animal morphology, ecology, and evolution—a theory which hinges on the nonexistence of griffins. Yet it is this theory rather than the medieval one which permits reliable prediction and effective control.

Again, the medieval scientist made assertions of the form (Ex) -Fx; an illustration of this assertion would be "Some entities do not obey the laws of terrestrial matter." He would put forward the case of the heavenly bodies, which he supposed to be made of an uncorruptible and spiritual substance. But such an existentially quantified proposition contributes nothing to our knowledge of the heavens or of their relationship to the earth. Copernicus, Galileo, and Newton were able to explain this relationship only by taking the risk of denying the existential proposition in question and thereby asserting a universal one. What they asserted was, in effect, that *everything* obeys the laws of terrestrial matter; this has the structure, (x) Fx. There are tremendous odds against such a generalization; the existence of one remote and solitary body stubbornly obeying its own laws rather than those of Newton would constitute evidence against the entire content of modern mechan-

ics.   Whether a modern scientist could, in the fact of those fundamental convictions from which he proceeds, acknowledge such
evidence is, of course, another question.

Let us rephrase 17.12 and 17.13 in the form of simple arguments.   There is no reason to proliferate terminology by assigning
these arguments distinct names.   It is important only to remember
the structures involved.   These are as follows:

(17.14) (x) $-Fx$
            $\overline{-(Ex)\ Fx}$

and

(17.15) (Ex) $-Fx$
            $\overline{-(x)\ Fx}$

One other significant relationship between universal and existential quantification should be observed.   Whenever a property belongs to everything in the universe, it belongs to at least one entity
in the universe, although the converse of this is by no means true.
Thus "(x) $Fx \rightarrow (Ex)$ Fx" is a logical truth, which might be expressed in the form of the argument

(17.16) (x) Fx
            $\overline{(Ex)\ Fx}$

Of (x) Fx and (Ex) $-Fx$," one must be true and the other
false; therefore, they are *contradictories* of each other. (Ex) Fx
and (x) $-Fx$ are likewise contradictories.   The propositions (x)
Fx and (x) $-Fx$ are, on the other hand, contraries only; not both
of them could be true at the same time, but both might well be
false.

The relations of contrary and contradictory just noted bear
strong resemblances to those among the traditional standard forms.
But this does not mean that any of the forms we have so far discussed is that of the *A*-, *I*-, *O*-, or *E*-propositions.   The latter
are, in fact, sharply to be distinguished from the former, because
each of them expresses a relationship between *two* classes.   Forms

such as (x) Fx and $-(Ex)$ $Fx,$ on the other hand, are concerned with no more than *one* class at a time, namely, F. This raises the problem of adequately expressing the more complicated standard forms in the notation of quantification theory.

The I proposition, "Some F is G" means that at least one entity is both F and G. "Some Senators are Pennsylvanians," for example, is equivalent to the proposition, "At least one entity is both Senator and a Pennsylvanian." Thus

(17.17) I has the structure (Ex) $(Fx \& Gx)$.

Similarly,

(17.18) O has the structure (Ex) $(Fx \& - Gx),$

since "Some F is not G" means "There is something which is F but not G." The existential quantifier occurring in 17.17 and 17.18 reflects the existential import of these propositions.

E is the contradictory of I; therefore its quantificational structure is that of the denial of the structure of I. It follows that

(17.19) E has the structure, $-(Ex)$ $(Fx \& Gx)$.

This may be written in the equivalent form (x) $-(Fx \& Gx)$, or, by the definitions of Section 10 (page 75), (x) $Fx \rightarrow -Gx)$. If no F is G, it follows that whatever x we choose, if it is F, it is not G.

Finally, A is the contradictory of O, so that it may be symbolized $-(Ex)$ $(Fx \& -Gx)$. It is clearer, however, to transform this into (x) $-(Fx \& -Gx)$. The definition of implication in terms of conjunction and negation shows, in turn, that

(17.20) A has the structure, (x) $(Fx \rightarrow Gx)$.

It is 17.20 to which we should give especial attention; in particular, we should notice its hypothetical or conditional force. Not only does 17.20 express the logical structure of an A-proposition which has no existential import, but also, and more significantly, 17.20 is the form of any scientific law. A law differs from a generalization such as "There are no griffins" in that it relates two or more classes of objects.   An example of a law is that which relates freely falling objects to objects which obey the formula "*s* equals one-half *g* times the square of *t*."   For the scientist does not wish to assert that *every* entity obeys this law; he means it to apply only to those which are *falling freely*.   Thus all that he is prepared to defend is the proposition "Whatever entity you choose, if it falls, it does so according to this formula."   All that this means, in turn, is that *no* entity can fall *without* behaving according to the formula in question; it does not, however, mean that every object, or any object, is falling.   For similar reasons every scientific law has a conditional structure.   No phenomenon may be said without qualification to behave in a given way; and the stipulation of the appropriate qualification is always the antecedent of a universally quantified conditional.

The fundamental structural dissimilarity between the *A* and the *I* should be not only noticed but also understood.   *I* must be the quantification of a conjunction rather than of a conditional, since (Ex) $(Fx \rightarrow Gx)$ is true for nearly every *F* and *G*, and does not therefore convey the precise information that (Ex) $(Fx$ & $Gx)$ does.   The proposition "There is some entity such that if it is a Senator, then it is a Pennsylvanian" is, in fact, trivial, because a Representative answers to the entity in question; a Representative is not a Senator, so that the conditional as a whole, having a false antecedent, is true.   For corresponding reasons, the *A*-proposition must be expressed structurally as a conditional rather than as a conjunction.   "All whales are mammals" means "For any entity selected, if it is a whale, it is a mammal"; but it does not mean "For any entity selected, it is a whale and it is a mammal."   The world is not wholly made up of cetaceans.

The version of the *A*-proposition which has existential import may be written $[(x)$ $(Fx \rightarrow Gx)]$ & $[(Ex)$ $Fx]$.   For if we are to argue from "All Communists advocate revolution" to the conclusion "Some Communists advocate revolution," we must supply the extra premise "There is at least one Communist." The structure of this argument is

(17.21) (x) $(Fx \rightarrow Gx)$
(Ex) Fx
$\overline{(Ex) \quad (Fx \ \& \ Gx)}$

If something is both round and red, then something is round and something is red. But if something is round and something is square, it does not follow that something is both round and square. In general,

(17.22) (Ex) $(Fx \ \& \ Gx) \rightarrow [(Ex) \ Fx \ \& \ (Ex) \ Gx]$,

while the converse of this is false. This raises the general question of the distribution of quantifiers throughout complex propositions. A complete and rigorous answer does not fall within the limits of this course. A partial reply is contained in the following conditionals and biconditionals:

(17.23) (x) $(Fx \ \& \ Gx) \longleftrightarrow [(x) \ Fx \ \& \ (x) \ Gx]$
(17.24) (Ex) $(Fx \ v \ Gx) \longleftrightarrow [(Ex) \ Fx \ v \ (Ex) \ Gx]$
(17.25) $[(x) \ Fx \ v \ (x) \ Gx] \rightarrow (x) \ (Fx \ v \ Gx)$
(17.26) (x) $(Fx \ v \ Gx) \rightarrow [(x) \ Fx \ v \ (Ex) \ Gx]$

According to 17.23, everything is spatial and temporal if, and only if, everything is spatial and everything is temporal. By 17.24, something is either above reproach or beneath contempt if, and only if, something is above reproach or something is beneath contempt. The conditionals just enumerated are, however, probably more illuminating than the biconditionals, because the unwarranted assertion of their converse is a source of confusion in everyday thinking. Thus by 17.25, if everything is material or everything is mental, then everything is material or mental; but it is not true that if everything is material or mental, then *everything* is material or *everything* is mental. As 17.26 tells us, the most we can conclude from the premise "Everything is material or mental" is "Everything is material or *something* is mental." Notice that when Fx and Gx are contradictories, 17.26 becomes the logical truth 17.2 mentioned earlier in this section. Because everything is either F or not F by virtue of the Law of the Excluded

Middle, it follows that either everything is F or something is not F.

By now it should be clear that quantification is a powerful and subtle analysis of logical truth which reaches far beyond the limitations of the syllogism or the propositional calculus. The importance of this technique is even more obvious when it is applied to relations of higher degree than the monadic. A few examples of what can be expressed when dyadic relations are quantified will bring this section to a conclusion.

A dyadic relation whose terms are x and y may be symbolized $F\ x\ y$. This may be read *"x bears the relation F to y."* Where F stands for "is the father of," $F\ x\ y$ means *"x is the father of y"*; where F represents "is greater than," $F\ x\ y$ means *"x is greater than y."* $F\ y\ x$, on the other hand, would be read *"y is the father of x,"* or *"y is greater than x."* Where F is symmetrical, of course, $F\ x\ y$ and $F\ y\ x$ have the same meaning. For instance, x sits next to y if, and only if, y sits next to x.

Among the possible quantifications of $F\ x\ y$ are the following:

(17.27) $(x)\ (y)\ F\ x\ y$
(17.28) $(y)\ (x)\ F\ x\ y$
(17.29) $(Ex)\ (y)\ F\ x\ y$
(17.30) $(y)\ (Ex)\ F\ x\ y$
(17.31) $(x)\ (Ey)\ F\ x\ y$
(17.32) $(Ey)\ (x)\ F\ x\ y$
(17.33) $(Ex)\ (Ey)\ F\ x\ y$
(17.34) $(Ey)\ (Ex)\ F\ x\ y$

The order of quantifiers in each of these propositions represents the order in which the variables are chosen or selected. Suppose, for example, that F represents the relation "is the cause of." Then 17.27 will mean "Whatever x you select, it is the cause of whatever y you then select"; on this interpretation 17.28 will signify "Whatever y you select, it is caused by whatever x you then select." These propositions are equivalent and, in general, when both quantifiers are universal, their order is irrelevant.

Order is, however, essential to the quantifiers occurring in the next four propositions. What 17.29 asserts is that at least one x

may be chosen such that x is the cause of whatever y may then be chosen.   This has often been taken as the fundamental premise of the Cosmological Argument, an argument intended as a proof that God is the cause of everything.   On the other hand, 17.30 alleges only that whatever y you chose, at least one cause may be assigned to it.   This is a basic thesis of ordinary natural science on which every event has a cause.   If 17.29 be read "Some fixed entity is the cause of every entity," and 17.30 as "Every entity is caused by some entity or other," the radical difference between them should be clear.

Similarly, 17.31 may be freely translated as "Every event has some effect or other," and 17.32 as "There is some fixed effect which every entity has."   The former is a criterion which one may employ to distinguish between appearance and reality: an event is real only if it has at least one subsequent effect.   The latter might well be asserted by those who believe that every event has the effect of attesting to the power of God.

There is, however, a relation of implication between 17.29 and 17.30 and between 17.32 and 17.31.   This relation can best be exhibited in terms of another illustration.   Let F represent "is a number greater than."   Then $(Ex)\ (y)\ F\ x\ y$ means, "Some fixed number is greater than every number."   But if this is true, then it follows that for every number one might select, there is at least one number greater than it, namely, the fixed number in question. So 17.29 implies 17.30.   For similar reasons 17.32 implies 17.31; if there is at least one fixed number such that every number is greater than it (and zero is, in fact, such a number), then it follows that whatever number one may choose, it is greater than at least one number (zero).   In general, the argument

$$(17.35)\quad \frac{(Ex)\ (y)\ Fx}{(y)\ (Ex)\ Fx}$$

is possible, although the converse of the argument does not follow from it.

This argument has surprising results for the example of causation used above. For on it, the theistic declaration "God is the cause of everything" implies the scientific principle "Everything has a cause." However it should be borne in mind that this latter proposition does not define science or exhaust its fundamental beliefs. In addition to the assumption that everything has a cause, the scientist assumes that different events have different causes and that the system of causes and effects operates according to specific laws. These added assumptions are not implied by "God is the cause of everything." Similarly, it is not sufficient for the mathematician to cite only zero as a number less than any given number; he must suppose that for each number greater than one, there are several smaller numbers. But this auxiliary supposition is not implied by "There is at least one fixed number such that every number is greater than it."

All that need be said about 17.33 and 17.34 is that, like 17.27 and 17.28, they are equivalent. When both quantifiers are existential, order is irrelevant.

Quantification, then, can discriminate among meanings whose difference is opaque to any other sort of analysis hitherto considered. But in this book we can do no more than touch its fringes. The general theory of quantification, developed by modern logicians, is a far-ranging and exacting enterprise, the consequences of which have not yet been fully developed.

EXERCISES

A. Using appropriate symbols for the classes involved, express each proposition occurring in Exercise D following Section 12 (pages 111-12) in the symbolism of quantification theory.

B. Express each of the following in quantificational symbolism, using Ax for "x is an atom," Mx for "x is in motion," and the other symbols suggested when necessary. Determine whether each argument is valid.

  1. Everything is made of atoms. Therefore, at least one thing is made of atoms.

2. Nothing is made of atoms. Therefore, at least one thing is made of atoms.
3. It is not the case that everything is made of atoms. Therefore, nothing is made of atoms.
4. It is not the case that everything is made of atoms. Therefore, at least one thing is not made of atoms.
5. It is not the case that at least one thing is not made of atoms. Therefore, at least one thing is made of atoms.
6. At least one thing is made of atoms. Therefore, it is not the case that at least one thing is not made of atoms.
7. At least one thing is not made of atoms. Therefore, it is not the case that everything is made of atoms.
8. Everything is made of atoms and is in motion. Therefore, everything is made of atoms and everything is in motion. (*Hint:* Consult 17.23-17.26.)
9. Everything is made of atoms or is in motion. Therefore, everything is made of atoms or everything is in motion.
10. Something is made of atoms and something is in motion. Therefore, something is made of atoms and is in motion.
11. Everything is made of atoms or is in motion. Therefore, everything is made of atoms or something is in motion.
12. All atoms are in motion. There is at least one atom. Therefore, there is at least one thing in motion. (*Hint:* Consult the discussion of 17.21.)
13. Everything is related to something. Therefore, there is something which is related to everything. (*Rxy*)
14. There is something which is related to everything. Therefore, everything is related to something. (*Rxy*)
15. Everything is related to everything. Therefore, there is something which is related to everything. (*Rxy*)

C. (a) Using the abbreviation *Sxy* for "person *x* speaks language *y*," symbolize the following propositions:

1. There are people who speak every language.
2. There exists a language which everyone speaks.
3. Anyone speaks some language or other.
4. Whatever language you choose, at least one person speaks it.
5. Someone speaks some language.
6. There are languages which no one speaks.
7. There are people who speak no language.

8. Everyone speaks every language.
9. Not everyone speaks every language.
10. Not every language is spoken by everyone.

(b) Which propositions in this list imply others in the list? Enumerate all such cases.

D. "Any x is F" means "Every x is F." But does "Not any x is F" mean "Not every x is F"? If not, what does it mean? What of "All x is F"? "Each x is F"?

SUPPLEMENTARY READINGS

1. W. V. Quine, *Methods of Logic*, New York, Henry Holt & Company, 1950, Secs. 16-32.
2. Irving M. Copi, *Introduction to Logic*, New York, The Macmillan Company, 1953, Ch. 10.

18

Fallacies

Up to this point we have been engaged in a discussion of logical ideas and techniques of continuously increasing complexity. The reader who has followed this development should by now be able in a general way to understand the significance of logic as a systematic field of study. His conception of the nature of logic ought to be much more precise than it was at the outset.

Elementary deductive logic as such will not, however, be elaborated any further in the succeeding pages of this book. Instead, we shall turn to matters of two sorts. The first is a brief survey of logical error—a survey which could not have been wholly meaningful had we not considered first the various forms of logical truth. This topic will occupy us in the present section. The second main topic yet to be treated is the relation between logic and knowledge in general; to this we shall address ourselves in Part Four.

If we were to take "logical error" in the broad sense, to include any mistake whatsoever in attempting to solve a logical problem—a mistake, for example, in shading a Venn Diagram or in assigning a truth-value in a truth-table—we should find the task of classifying such errors hopeless. There is no accounting in general for the errors of this sort that people are liable to make. What we shall be interested in, however, is nothing so inclusive. It is rather those general types of logical error which have most fre-

185

quently frustrated the attempt to argue validly.   In particular, we shall concentrate on arguments that *seem* plausible, but *are,* in fact, erroneous.   Such arguments are called *fallacies.*

Two claims of the arguer were noted in Section 5.   The first is that the premises *imply* the conclusion, and the second is that the conclusion may be *inferred* as a matter of independent information.   A general type of fallacy is associated with each of these claims.   Where the premises do no imply the conclusion, the fallacy falls under the broad heading of *non sequitur* (Latin for "it does not follow").   And where, for reasons of logic rather than merely of fact, the conclusion cannot be inferred, the fallacy is a species of *petitio principii* ("begging the question").   This phrase is often shortened to *petitio.*   "Arguing in a circle" is a synonym for this word.

All of the fallacies mentioned throughout the preceding pages are cases of *non sequitur* rather than of *petitio principii.*   For example, denying the antecedent, asserting the consequent, the fallacies of alternation and conjunction, the fallacious conversion of *A-* and *O*-propositions, and the fallacies of illicit process and four terms connected with the syllogism, alike illustrate *non sequitur,* since they are all instances in which the arguer's claim that the premises imply the conclusion is not justified.   Of course it is possible for an arguer to be guilty of *non sequitur* in many other ways as well, including ways that it would not even be profitable to symbolize.   An argument such as

(18.1)   The hydrogen bomb is capable of destroying civilization
───
          Man should turn away from science and toward religion

contains so many implicit assumptions that it is impossible to ascertain, merely by inspecting it, what logical structure (if any) it is supposed to have.   As it stands, the argument is just an amorphous *non sequitur;* the conclusion clearly does not follow from the single premise given.   But it is conceivable that if the speaker were to make all of his assumptions clear, the result would be formally valid.   The process of clarification which would be necessary, however, answers to no technique of deductive logic in itself. The standards of clarity in exposition must rather be sought in such fields as English composition, public speaking, and semantics. Strictly speaking, the identification of a logical fallacy presupposes that the argument so identified is already clearly and completely stated.

Some of the cases of *non sequitur* which we have been able to symbolize, however, differ from other cases in an important way. Almost all of the fallacies which were explicitly mentioned in the preceding pages were *invalid* arguments—denying the antecedent, arguing from an *A*-proposition to its converse, and using a syllogism with a term distributed in the conclusion but not in the premises, are illustrations. Each of these examples has the specious appearance of a valid argument.

However, certain fallacies associated with the syllogism do not fall within the category of invalid arguments; these are the fallacy of four terms and its two special cases, the fallacies of composition and division. A cursory glance at 15.5, 15.6, and 15.7 (page 155) shows that they are all valid structures; each, in fact, is *AAA* in the 1st figure. The fallaciousness of these arguments does not, therefore, reside in their structure. It is, rather, a matter of the way in which this structure is embodied in a particular context of ordinary words. The difficulty is that some of the words are ambiguous. There are "four terms" because in each of its occurrences the middle term has a different meaning; but this difference is not revealed by the symbols we have adopted to express the form of the syllogism.

Arguments which are formally valid, but conclusions of which fail to follow from their premises, owing to an ambiguity, may be called *fallacies of equivocation*. These are contrasted with *formal fallacies,* which are formally invalid. Both formal fallacies and those of equivocation are, in this classification, species of *non sequitur*.

There are many types of ambiguity capable of leading to fallacies of equivocation. Six were mentioned by Aristotle, who first proposed a classification of fallacies similar to the present one.* The number of fallacies reported by modern investigators is much greater than this.   But the investigation itself is not properly a part of deductive logic; it belongs rather to such studies as rhetoric and semantics.   For our purposes it is sufficient to add that fallacies of this kind are by no means peculiar to syllogisms. They may, in fact, arise in connection with any sort of valid argument.   Consider the immediate inference

(18.2)   All humans are entities.

No human is a nonentity.

While this expresses the correct obversion of an *A*-proposition, its conclusion is misleading.   An entity is anything whatever that exists.   But a nonentity is not something that doesn't exist; it is rather a person or thing *without worth*.   Although the proposition that no human is worthless is regarded by many as true, it does not follow merely from the premise that humans exist.

The following argument is a fallacy of equivocation within the logic of propositions:

(18.3)   If it is raining, Boggs does not tell the truth.

It is raining.

Boggs does not tell the truth.

The danger in this valid conditional argument is that the conclusion is apt to be taken as expressing a general trait of Boggs's character rather than an isolated incident in a perhaps otherwise impeccable career.   In the first premise, "Boggs does not tell the truth" acquires its meaning in relation to the particular antecedent of which it is the consequent.   Thus it must retain this meaning in the conclusion, which ought therefore to be interpreted "Boggs does not tell the truth *about the present weather*."

A famous fallacy of equivocation which occurs in John Stuart Mill's *Utilitarianism* may be paraphrased as a chain argument

---

* See Ralph M. Eaton, *General Logic*, New York, Charles Scribner's Sons, 1931, pp. 333-34, for Aristotle's classification.

(although this is by no means the only way in which it may be analyzed).

(18.4) If happiness is desired, it is desirable.
  If it is desirable, it is good.
  ─────────────────────────────
  If happiness is desired, it is good.*

The trouble is, of course, that in the first premise "desirable" is intended to mean "capable of being desired" (as "visible" means "capable of being seen"), while in the second premise it has the force of "worthy of being desired" (as "admirable" means "worthy of being admired").

Having sketched some of the main ways in which an argument may be a *non sequitur* (having a conclusion which its premises fail to imply), let us turn to *petitio,* an argument in which it is impossible to infer the conclusion. We must stress at the outset that this class of fallacies is not intended to include cases where the impossibility of inferring the conclusion is merely the result of the factual falsity of the premises. The conclusion of any argument can be avoided, provided that some or all of its premises can be shown to be false. For we cannot *infer* the conclusion unless we can *assert* all of the premises. Thus we can avoid the necessity of accepting the conclusion of a dilemma either by taking it by the horns—denying the truth of its major premise—or by escaping between the horns—denying the minor premise. The fact that we cannot infer the conclusion of an argument from its premises is no proof, of course, that the conclusion could not be demonstrated as the valid consequence of another set of premises, which might be inescapably true. It only proves that the conclusion cannot be inferred from the premises *at hand,* since to assert them would be improper. But this situation does not in itself stigmatize any argument as a fallacy. A dilemma is not a fallacy merely because its conclusion is avoidable; nor is a syllogism, or alternative argument, or any other valid argument, the truth of whose

─────────────────

* For the original context and statement of this argument, see *Utilitarianism,* beginning of Chapter IV.

various premises may almost always be challenged. The impossibility of inferring the conclusion is symptomatic of a *fallacy* only when that impossibility is logical and not merely factual.

This is the case when the conclusion itself is either implicitly or explicitly contained among the premises which are represented as implying it. Another name for "inference" is "proof," and, as was pointed out in Section 5 (page 26), nothing is proved merely by asserting it. To prove a proposition, one must assert not *it,* but rather those premises which *imply* it. But if the conclusion is one of the premises, in asserting the latter one has automatically asserted the former without proof. Thus the supposed *proof* of the conclusion, which is presumably the result of asserting the premises, is gratuitous.

Let us get down to cases. Imagine that Meggs and Suggs are discussing Meggs's most recent love affair:

MEGGS: She loves me.
SUGGS: How do you know?
MEGGS: She told me so.
SUGGS: What makes you think she's telling the truth?
MEGGS: She wouldn't lie to me, because she loves me.

But this last statement only proves the muddled condition of Meggs's mind. He has assumed precisely what he had set out to prove.

A more literary case of *petitio* is that exposed by the philosopher David Hume in the following passage (Hume is questioning a supposed proof of the thesis that every event must have a cause):

Every thing, 'tis said, must have a cause; for if any thing wanted a cause, *it* wou'd produce *itself;* that is, exist before it existed; which is impossible. But this reasoning is plainly inconclusive; because it supposes, that in our denial of a cause we still grant what we expressly deny, *viz.,* that there must be a cause; which therefore is taken to be the object itself. . . . [But to exclude] all external causes, excludes *a fortiori* the thing itself which is created. An object, that exists absolutely without any cause, certainly is not its own cause.*

* *A Treatise of Human Nature* (Ed. Selby-Bigge), Oxford, Clarendon Press, 1888, pp. 80-81.

A third example of *petitio* arose recently in connection with the much-debated question of whether Shakespeare actually wrote the plays attributed to him. Some critics doubt that he did, on the ground that he was not sufficiently well educated to have possessed all the knowledge displayed in the plays. A prominent scholar replied, however, that *the plays themselves reveal that Shakespeare was an educated man!* But this answer clearly assumes precisely what is at issue; to wit, that Shakespeare wrote the plays.

Any *petitio* is, of course, a valid argument, in the sense that it is tautologously true. Its defect is only that of being *too* valid; of not providing a structure into which independent facts can be fitted so as to yield a new fact as a conclusion. *Petitio* can be symbolized in the following manner:

(18.5) q

p

r

$\overline{}$

p

This is logically true no matter what q and r happen to be, and, for that matter, no matter how many additional premises are conjoined with them. For whenever a conjunct is true, it follows that one of its members (namely, the conclusion p) is true.

Associated with *petitio* is the so-called *fallacy of many questions*. This fallacy consists in asking a question, the significance of which may depend upon a point that has not been established or agreed upon. Thus the public speaker who asks "Why is there such a mess in Washington?" assumes that there *is* a mess in Washington; the mere question, however, does not constitute a proof that there is. Before asking *why p* is true, it is always well to show *that p* is true. Another form of the fallacy of many questions is the oldest of logical chestnuts: "Have you stopped beating your wife yet?"

EXERCISE

(a) Which of the following arguments are fallacious?

(b) Identify each fallacy as *non sequitur* or *petitio*.

(c) Identify each *non sequitur* as a formal fallacy or a fallacy of equivocation.

(d) Identify each formal fallacy, where possible, by its standard name.

(e) In the case of each fallacy of equivocation, identify the words or words used ambiguously, and define the different meanings involved.

1. If I am lucky, I will catch the train.
   If I do not catch the train, I will hitchhike.

   If I am lucky, I will hitchhike.   (L,T,H)

2. If I am lucky, I will catch the train.
   If I do not catch the train, I will hitchhike.

   If I do not catch the train, I am out of luck.

3. All cases of *non sequitur* are fallacious.
   Some cases of *non sequitur* are valid.

   Some valid arguments are fallacious.

4. All cases of *non sequitur* are fallacious.
   Some cases of *non sequitur* are not valid.

   Some valid arguments are not fallacious.

5. If I press this switch, the mountainside will blow up.
   And if the mountainside blows up, the entire county will hear it.   Thus if I press the switch, the entire county will hear it.

6. Normal activities are those which are proper.   But what the average person does is normal.   Therefore, what the average person does is proper.

7. No genius is normal.   Hence, all geniuses are abnormal.

8. It is rational to suppose that every event has a cause. For even if some men deny it, they could not deny it if they were rational.

9. Hot dogs are better than nothing.
   Nothing is better than steak.

   Hot dogs are better than steak.

10. Whoever believes that men should have all things in common is a communist.
    Many monks believe that men should have all things in common.

    Many monks are Communists.

11. Every statement in this book is true.   And the authority for this is that "Every statement in this book is true" is, after all, a statement in this book.

12. Every integer is finite. But the number of all integers is not finite. Therefore, the number of all integers is not an integer.

13. To call you an animal is to speak the truth. And to call you a jackass is to call you an animal. Therefore, to call you a jackass is to speak the truth.

14. All humans have moral potentialities.

   No humans have immoral potentialities.

15. Boggs takes Composition if he is a freshman. But he is not a freshman. So he does not take Composition.

16. Boggs is a fraternity man unless he is a freshman. But he is not a freshman. So he is a fraternity man.

17. Why are men better drivers than women? Is this due to an innate lack of capacity, or merely to inexperience? It is only in the latter case that we can hope to improve the situation.

18. Men are better drivers than women because they are more competent at handling a car on the road.

19. If a simple dilemma is constructive, it is valid, and if it is destructive, it is valid.

   It must be either constructive or destructive.

   A simple dilemma is valid.

20. All arguments having all true premises and a false conclusion are invalid.

   Argument No. 20 on this page has all true premises and a false conclusion.

   Argument No. 20 on this page is invalid.

   (*Hint:* What word or words do you think are being used ambiguously in this argument? Don't worry if your answer is not conclusive; no logician has yet been able to give a conclusive answer.)

21. All brothers have the same father.

   The brother of Meggs and the brother of Diggs are brothers.

   The brother of Meggs and the brother of Diggs have the same father.

22. Some automobiles are not green. Hence, some green things are not automobiles.

23. Any ruler who assumes powers not natural to his office is a dictator.

   Roosevelt assumed powers not natural to his office (for example, during the war).

   Roosevelt was a dictator.

24. *The World Almanac* is a phrase of fifteen letters. All the

events of the year are reported in *The World Almanac*. Therefore, all the events of the year are reported in a phrase of
fifteen letters.

25. Hoboken is the fairest city of the land.   And whoever denies
this is simply not competent to judge.   For the belief that
Hoboken *is* the fairest city is a necessary condition for competence in these matters.

26. I have just asked you whether you intended to kill the deceased,
and you have denied it.   By your own statement, then, you are
guilty of unpremeditated murder.

27. An elephant is an animal.
    _____
    A gray elephant is a gray animal.
    (*Hint:* The basis for evaluating this argument was not stated in
    this book.   But whether it is valid or not should be obvious.)

28. An elephant is an animal.
    _____
    A small elephant is a small animal.

29. Frenchmen are a nation.
    Burgundians are Frenchmen.
    _____
    Burgundians are a nation.

30. Assuming that x plus 0 equals x, it can easily be shown that
there is no other number except 0 such that, when it is added
to x, the sum is x.   For suppose there were two such numbers;
call them 0_1 and 0_2.   Then, on the assumption we have just
made,

$$0_1 \text{ plus } 0_2 \text{ equals } 0_1$$

and $$0_1 \text{ plus } 0_2 \text{ equals } 0_2$$

Since things equal to the same thing are equal to each other, it
follows that 0_1 equals 0_2; or, in other words, there are not 2
numbers of the sort in question.

SUPPLEMENTARY READINGS

1. W. Stanley Jevons, *Lessons in Logic,* London, Macmillan and
Co., 1893, Lessons XX-XXI.

2. Ralph M. Eaton, *General Logic,* New York, Charles Scribner's
Sons, 1931, Pt. II, Ch. IV.

3. Morris R. Cohen and Ernest Nagel, *An Introduction to Logic and
Scientific Method,* New York, Harcourt, Brace and Company, Inc.,
1934, Ch. XIX.

4. W. H. Werkmeister, *An Introduction to Critical Thinking,* Lincoln, Nebraska, Johnsen Publishing Company, 1948, Pt. I, Chs. II-III.

5. Herbert L. Searles, *Logic and Scientific Methods,* New York, The Ronald Press Company, 1948, Ch. 9.

PART FOUR

Postulates

19

The Formal Properties of Sets
of Postulates

A central point made in Section 5 was that nothing can be *proved* unless something else is *assumed*. For conclusions require premises; a proposition merely asserted without being exhibited as the consequence of assumptions already acknowledged can make no fundamental appeal to our reason. In the last two parts of this book we have been concerned with the logical consequences of various combinations of premises; we have thus been investigating the forms which proofs may validly assume. But we have so far ignored the properties of assumptions or premises in themselves, apart from the particular arguments in which they figure. To these, in their most general aspects, we turn now.

An assumption or premise viewed primarily as necessary to proof is often spoken of as a *postulate* or *axiom*. A postulate is thus whatever proposition is assumed in order that others may be proved. Postulates occur in all orderly disciplines: mathematics, physics, chemistry, and biology—each has its peculiar postulates. The Postulate of Parallels, the Inverse Square Law, Avogadro's Hypothesis, and Mendel's Laws come to mind as familiar examples. Less obvious instances of postulates will be cited shortly.

The detailed arguments involved in rational disciplines usually depend upon more than one postulate; geometry, for example, requires assumptions other than the Postulate of Parallels alone, and many postulates over and above that of Avogadro are essential to chemistry. It is thus fruitful to consider together the postulates fundamental to a given field. Such a basic group of assumptions is called a *set of postulates*. Newton's four laws are a set of postulates for mechanics, and Mendel's Laws for a simple part of genetics.

Now the most significant formal properties of postulates are those expressing the relations among the members of a set. These properties include *consistency, independence,* and *completeness*. A set of postulates is *consistent* when no postulate in it is the contradictory of another and no consequence, or theorem, can be derived from the postulates in question so as to contradict any other theorem. If, on the other hand, there is any proposition *p* such that both *p* and -*p* can be proved on the basis of the set of postulates in question, the set is inconsistent.

Two propositions are in general *independent* if neither implies the other. When more than two postulates comprise a set, any given one of them is independent of the others if the conjunct of the others does not imply it. In such a way, all of the postulates forming a given set might be independent.

A set of postulates is *complete* when it implies every possible true statement which can be phrased in terms of the elements at hand. The axioms and postulates from which plane geometry is derived, for instance, would form a complete set if every true proposition about the relationships among points, angles, lines, congruence, and so on, could be proved as a theorem. A complete set of axioms for mechanics would imply every true proposition connecting forces with spatial relations. If a complete set of postulates for algebra could be stated, this would warrant all truths about the relationships of numbers. Departing somewhat from conventional illustrations of postulate-sets, we may characterize a legal code as complete when from it, the lawfulness or unlawfulness of any act can be deduced. The example of the set of rules for a game may also be adduced; this, too, is a postulate-set, and is complete if any possible move or play of the game can be interpreted according to it. If the referee in a football game could find no rule on which to base one or another of his decisions, this would mean that the rulebook was incomplete.

The relationship between completeness, independence, and consistency may be summarized in a single formula: A set of postulates or axioms is *complete* when it is impossible to add any *independent* axiom or postulate to it without creating a new set which is *inconsistent*. In order to make this formula clear, however, it is desirable to discuss a concrete example.

The rules of the syllogism constitute a simple set of postulates. This set is complete because it permits us quite unambiguously to decide precisely which of the 256 possible moods of the syllogism are valid. Thus every true proposition about the validity of syllogisms is implied by the set. The rules of the syllogism are, furthermore, consistent. There is no proposition derivable from them, the contradictory of which is also derivable. For example, it does not follow from these rules that *AOO* in the 3rd figure is both valid and invalid. If this, or any similar contradiction could be derived, the rules would be inconsistent.

Suppose now that we wished to add one more rule to this set. Because the set is complete, any additional rule we can produce will either be a theorem or the contradictory of a theorem. For instance, the supplementary rule "The middle term cannot be distributed twice" is a theorem derivable from the original set, while the rule "The middle term may be distributed twice" is the contradictory of this theorem. Now if a rule which is already a theorem were added to the set, this new rule could not be independent of the others. It could be independent only if it were not a theorem. But a rule is not a theorem only when it contradicts a theorem. If such a rule were added, the set of rules would then become inconsistent, because both a certain theorem and its contradictory could be derived from it. Thus an independent axiom or postulate can be added to a complete set only at the expense of rendering the set inconsistent.

For the reader who, having threaded his way through the preceding portions of this book, has come to feel that a certain amount of clarity is gained in the use of symbols rather than ordinary language, a symbolic restatement of the definitions of the properties of postulate-sets may be welcomed. Where there is a set of postulates P_1, P_2 . . . , P_m, which together imply a group of theorems T_1, T_2, . . . T_n, the relation between the postulates and the theorems may be expressed as

(19.1) $(P_1 \& P_2 \& \ . \ . \ . \ \& P_m) \to (T_1 \& T_2 \& \ . \ . \ . \ \& T_n)$.

The reiterated "&"s in 19.1 take cognizance of the fact that all members of a set of postulates are simultaneously asserted to be true; and the same applies to the theorems.

The entire group of P's and T's may be referred to as the *system* (for example, the system of mechanics, the system of plane geometry, and so forth). If the postulates are to serve as a useful formulation of the system, n must be considerably greater than m; for if a relatively large number of assumptions must be made in order to prove a relatively small number of conclusions, the chances are that the body of propositions in question is not itself sufficiently well organized to permit fruitful analysis into postulates and theorems. Examples might be cited from many of the so-called "social sciences" in their present stage of development.

We may now give symbolic definitions of each of the three formal properties of sets of postulates.

(19.2) "P_1, P_2, . . . , P_m are *independent*" means
"-$[(P_1 \& P_2 \& \ . \ . \ . \ \& P_{m-1}) \to P_m]$ and -$[(P_2 \& P_3 \& \ . \ . \ . \ \& P_m) \to P_1]$ and -$[(P_1 \& P_3 \& \ . \ . \ . \ \& P_m) \to P_2]$, and so on."

(19.3) "P_1, P_2, . . . , P_m are *consistent*" means
"There is no T such that $(P_1 \& P_2 \& \ . \ . \ . \ \& P_m) \to (T \& \text{-}T)$."

(19.4) "P_1, P_2, . . . , P_m are *complete*" means
"Any independent P_{m+1} conjoined with them would yield an inconsistent set."

None of these definitions, however, is intended here as the basis for the *proof* of any further formula. The function of 19.1-19.4 is only to explicate ideas already discussed in the text.

Completeness is an ideal of all human knowledge, for the communication of facts or evaluations collapses whenever it is asserted that there are truths independent of one's fundamental assumptions. The imperative to make all truth accessible to human thought has been the occasion of much philosophical concern; rationalism and empiricism alike claim complete sets of assumptions in which nothing is vague or dark. And it is the conviction of the materialist that all real features of the world are implied by the laws he asserts. All of these positions are motivated, at least in part, by the demand for communication; all of them attempt to meet this demand by pursuing the ideal of completeness.

One technical detail which stands in the way of this pursuit is that general methods have as yet to be devised for testing either the completeness or the consistency of sets of postulates. In practice, we discover the inconsistency of a set when we are able to deduce contradictory theorems from it. But when the postulates together imply an indefinitely large number of theorems, it is often a matter of sheer luck to find two which contradict each other, and thus unrivaled optimism is required to claim that no two are contradictories. Similarly, it would usually be necessary to express all the possible truths about the elements related by a given set of postulates in order to show that none of these truths is independent of the set, and thus that the set is complete. Fortunately, there is a general method of testing for independence, and one which is simple enough to be outlined and applied within the limits of this book.

A proposition is independent of the set of which it is a member when it is not implied by any other member or any conjunction of other members. If p, q, and r form an independent set of postulates, then, as 19.2 indicates, the following relations will obtain:

(19.5) $-((p \ \& \ q) \rightarrow r)$
(19.6) $-((p \ \& \ r) \rightarrow q)$
(19.7) $-(r \ \& \ q) \rightarrow p)$

The first of these states that "r" is independent if the conditional "$(p \ \& \ q) \rightarrow r$" is false. This is equivalent to asserting that the contrapositive of the conditional must be false, or

(19.8) $-(-r \rightarrow -(p \ \& \ q))$

Expressing "$-(p \ \& \ q)$" in terms of alternation, we have

(19.9) $-(-r \rightarrow (-p \ \mathrm{v} \ -q)$

Thus r is independent unless its denial implies either the denial of p, or the denial of q, or both. To test the independence of r, then, we have only to deny it and see whether this denial rules out any other postulate. Let us forthwith apply this test to the rules of the syllogism. These rules are

1. If both premises are negative, there is no conclusion.
2. If one premise is negative, the conclusion is negative.
3. If both premises are universal, the conclusion is universal.
4. The middle term must be distributed at least once.
5. Any term distributed in the conclusion must have been distributed in a premise.

In order to prove these rules independent we have only to show that each in turn may be violated without affecting the others. For example,

(19.10) No M is P
         No S is M
         ———————
         No S is P

violates 1 while conforming to all the requirements dictated by 2, 3, 4, and 5. Therefore 1 is independent of the rest. So is 2, because

(19.11) No M is P
         All S is M
         ———————
         All S is P

violates 2 alone. The student may frame for himself the requisite examples to show that 3, 4, and 5 are likewise independent.

A word remains to be said about *equivalence*. Two sets of axioms or postulates are equivalent when every axiom or postulate of one is either a theorem or axiom or postulate of the other, and vice versa. Thus the complete system of postulates and theorems must be precisely the same for both sets. It follows from this that in order to be equivalent, two sets must be equally complete. Either both sets must be complete, or the propositions independent of one must be just those independent of the other.

It can be shown* that the following set of rules for the syllogism is equivalent with the set 1-5 adopted in this book:

1'. If both premises are particular, there is no conclusion.
2'. If one premise is particular, the conclusion is particular.
3'. If both premises are affirmative, the conclusion is affirmative.
4'. The middle term must be undistributed at least once.
5'. Any term undistributed in the conclusion must be undistributed in the premises.

This means that each of 1'-5' can be proved as a theorem on the basis of 1-5 (and indeed 1', 2', and 3' were proved in Section 15); it means also that each of 1-5 follows as a theorem from 1'-5'. In both cases the total system, comprising postulates and theorems, is the same. And, in view of the fact that 1-5 is complete, so is 1'-5'.

EXERCISES

A. Complete the proof that Rules 1-5 for the syllogism are all independent.

B. Prove that Rules 1'-5' given at the end of the present section are independent.

(*Hint:* This cannot be done if Rules 1-5 are assumed at the same time. Remember that if 1'-5' are taken to be the postulates for

* By the author, in an article to appear in a forthcoming number of *Philosophy of Science.*

the theory of the syllogism, Rules 1-5 lose their status as postulates and become theorems.)

C. When ">" is read as "is greater than," then the following postulates express some of the fundamental relationships among the integers:

> (a) If $x > y$, then x and y are different
> (b) If x and y are different, then either $x > y$ or $y > x$
> (c) If $x > y$ and $y > z$, then $x > z$

Prove that these three postulates are independent by showing that for each in turn there is a way of reading ">" so that that postulate will be false while the other two are still true.   (For example, if ">" in (b) is interpreted to mean "is an ancestor of," then (b) is false, but (a) and (b) are still true.)

D. Apply the procedure described in Exercise C, above, to determine whether the following postulates are independent:

> (a) $x = x$
> (b) If $x = y$, then $y = x$
> (c) If $x = y$ and $y = z$, then $x = z$

E. When all the members of a set of postulates can be significantly expressed in subject–predicate form, and when a small number of classes is involved, Venn Diagrams can be used to test the set for consistency.   Such a set is inconsistent when a star must fall within a shaded area; otherwise, it is consistent.   Determine whether the following set of postulates, describing in part the curriculum requirements of a certain college, is consistent:

> (a) All who take physics must take calculus.
> (b) Some who do not take calculus may take algebra.
> (c) But none may take both calculus and algebra.
> (d) All who take algebra must take physics.

F. A certain forward-looking organization has the following constitution.

> (a) Membership in the Society is restricted to those who have set foot on the planet Mars.

(b) All members are expected to give lectures on various phases of space travel.

(c) Only members of the Society will give such lectures.

1. Is this constitution consistent?
2. If, to (a), (b), and (c) there is added the further statement, *No visitor to Mars has joined the Society,* is the resulting set still consistent?
3. According to this resulting set, how many people are members of the Society?
4. According to this resulting set, how many people have given lectures on various phases of space travel?
5. Can it be deduced from this resulting set that no one has visited Mars?

G. The following postulates describe the members of a choral group.

(a) All who can sing tenor can sing baritone.
(b) Some who can read music cannot sing baritone.
(c) Some who can sing baritone can sing tenor.
(d) Some who can sing baritone cannot sing tenor.
(e) No one who can sing baritone can read music.

1. Is this set consistent?
2. Is it complete? (Is it possible to add to the set any further *independent* proposition in subject–predicate form which involves two of the three classes in question, but which is at the same time *consistent* with the set?)
3. Are postulates (a)-(e) independent? (How is independence manifested by Venn Diagrams?)
4. What is the minimum number of members which the group must have?
5. Can anyone read music? Who?

H. 1. If a set of postulates is inconsistent, is it necessarily incomplete? Explain.

2. If one postulate turns out to be not independent of the others, does that necessarily mean that the set is incomplete? Explain.

3. Suppose that two propositions are inconsistent with each other. Could they still be independent? Explain.

(*Hint:* Use A and O as examples.)

4. In the Propositional Calculus, are there any independent propositions?   Explain.

(*Hint:* Write out the truth-table for $-(p \rightarrow q)$ & $-(q \rightarrow p)$.)

5. Are all inconsistent sets of postulates equivalent?   Explain.

SUPPLEMENTARY READINGS

1. Morris R. Cohen and Ernest Nagel, *An Introduction to Logic and Scientific Method,* New York, Harcourt, Brace and Company, Inc., 1934, Ch. VII.

2. Alfred Tarski, *Introduction to Logic and to the Methodology of Deductive Sciences,* New York, Oxford University Press, 1941, Sec. 36; Secs. 38-42.

3. R. D. Carmichael, *The Logic of Discovery,* Chicago, The Open Court Publishing Co., 1930, Chs. I-III.

4. John Cooley, *A Primer of Formal Logic,* New York, The Macmillan Company, 1942, Ch. 7.

20

Postulates and Definitions

The fact that any proposition belonging to a set of postulates may only be a theorem derivable from an equivalent set suggests that a certain general misunderstanding about axioms or postulates may now be dispelled.   Throughout the ages it was thought that certain propositions had a peculiar claim to be the cornerstones of systems of knowledge.   Euclid's axioms and postulates, for example, were held to be self-evidently true, while the theorems which they implied were not considered to share the intuitive quality of their truth.   The millennium-long investigation which, in the nineteenth century, resulted in Lobachevski's proof that the Postulate of Parallels is independent of the rest, and in the founding of non-Euclidean geometry as a consequence, originated in the suspicion that this postulate was not sufficiently self-evident.   From a modern viewpoint, however, we can see that self-evidence is not a consideration in the choice of postulates.   All that the purposes of systematic knowledge demand is that the set we choose be consistent and complete; and many sets for a given discipline are equivalent in these respects.   Geometrical research in the twentieth century has produced many equivalent sets of postulates for Euclidean geometry, and from each of these one or more of Euclid's "self-evident" postulates may be deduced as a theorem. Given the appropriate assumptions, it is even possible to *prove* that a straight line is the shortest distance between two points.

Until the latter part of the nineteenth century it was believed that the fundamental truths of arithmetic, such as "two plus two equals four," had a privileged status in human knowledge by virtue of their self-evidence. The great German philosopher Immanuel Kant felt obligated to account for the peculiar prestige of these axioms as well as those of geometry, and so proposed that they were "synthetic *a priori* truths"—propositions conveying information about the structure of space and time but dependent for their truth upon no feature of the observable world. We know today that neither geometry nor arithmetic is synthetic in the sense of conveying information. The conceivability of an indefinitely large number of non-Euclidean geometries shows that the particular geometry expounded by Euclid not only is not based on postulates which are "self-evident" in any important sense, but also is not uniquely privileged to describe objective spatial relations. Nor does arithmetic have anything to say about the actual world. The monumental work of Bertrand Russell and Alfred North Whitehead in *Principia Mathematica* (1910-1913) tends to show that all arithmetical truths are analytic; being wholly expressible in terms of the logic of propositions and classes, they are true for all possible worlds. This shows that their "self-evidence" has no further significance than that of any logically true proposition, and in particular that the axioms of arithmetic are no more "self-evident" than the theorems.

In *Principia Mathematica,* Whitehead and Russell developed the propositional calculus from a set of independent postulates. They were forced to employ this postulational method for testing the validity of propositional arguments simply because no other was known at this time; the method of truth-tables was not proposed until 1921-22, by the logicians Wittgenstein and Post. A postulational approach to the logic of propositions is, however, useful for illustrating the relationship between postulates and theorems in equivalent sets. The sets we shall now produce are not those of Whitehead and Russell, and are far from complete, but they will serve our present purpose of exemplification.

(20.1) Postulate 1: $p \vee -p$

Postulate 2: $(p \vee q) \longleftrightarrow -(-p \;\&\; -q)$

Theorem 1: $-(p \;\&\; -p)$

Proof: Substitute $-p$ for q in Postulate 2.

This yields $(p \vee -p) \longleftrightarrow -(-p \;\&\; --p)$.

Applying the Law of Double Negation to cancel "$--$," and rearranging the right side of the equivalence, we obtain $(p \vee -p) \longleftrightarrow -(p \;\&\; -p)$.

But since the left side of this biconditional is true, by Postulate 1, so is the right side, or $-(p \;\&\; -p)$ Q.E.D.

(20.2) Postulate 1': $-(p \;\&\; -p)$

Postulate 2': $(p \;\&\; q) \longleftrightarrow -(-p \vee -q)$

Theorem 1': $p \vee -p$

Proof: Precisely analogous to that of Theorem 1 of set 20.1

The important feature of these two equivalent sets is that Postulate 1 of 20.1 is Theorem 1' of 20.2 and Postulate 1' of 20.2 is Theorem 1 of 20.1. Exactly the same relationship would be exhibited by another example we have already considered—the equivalent sets of rules for the syllogism, 1-5 and 1'-5'. For all of the rules of each set can be demonstrated as theorems implied by the other set. Both of these cases illustrate the point we are about to make: *No proposition has any peculiar claim to be a postulate rather than a theorem.* The thesis may also be stated positively: *The status of any proposition as a postulate or theorem is always relative to the system in which it occurs.* We shall identify this feature of systematic knowledge as *Postulational Relativity.*

Systems of knowledge also exhibit another significant sort of relativity which we shall uncover if we examine more closely the relationships among the elements with which various sets of postulates are concerned. Plane geometry is about points, lines, angles, congruence, and so on. Arithmetic deals with numbers, addition, and multiplication. Mechanics is concerned with the manipulations of vectors. The elements which the rules of the syllogism relate are syllogism, validity, middle term, negative premise, and

so forth. The propositional calculus is concerned with propositional variables and certain logical words. Thus each set of
postulates deals with a group of concepts, which may not be those
of another set. And each assumes that the *meanings* of at least
some of the concepts of which it treats are accessible to whoever
understands the postulates. Euclid assumed, for example, that
his public knew what he meant by a "point" and a "line"; mathe-
maticians suppose that when they use the word "addition," others
will know what they are talking about; and it seems clear that no
student will grasp the significance of sets 20.1 and 20.2 above,
unless he is clear as to the meanings of "v" and "&."

Not all of the concepts involved in a set of postulates, however,
need be assumed to be perfectly clear in meaning. Euclid did not
feel constrained to suppose that all of his contemporaries shared
his insight into the meaning of a "circle"; for he was able to define
"circle" in terms of the allegedly less obscure concepts of "point,"
"line," and "distance." The mathematician who is dubious that
his colleagues will understand by "subtraction" precisely what he
understands can *define* it as "the inverse of addition." And had it
been necessary to introduce new logical words into the system
common to 20.1 and 20.2, we could have done so by definition, as
indeed we did in Section 10. A simple and partial illustration of
the use of definitions within a set of postulates would, in fact,
be provided by schemes 10.2 and 10.3 in Section 10 (page 75);
here we defined all the other logical words first in terms of "v"
and "-"—the meanings of which we assumed—and then in terms
of "&" and "-."

Notice that *two* orders of definition were explicitly given in
Section 10 (page 75), and several others were mentioned. One
might define "→" in terms of "v" and "-," or "v" in terms of "→"
and "-." This sets the stage for the point we are now to make: *No
concept in itself has a clear and distinct meaning, and whether the
meaning of any concept is assumed or defined is relative to the
system in which the concept is employed.* This principle may be
called *Conceptual Relativity.*

A pair of equivalent sets of postulates will generally exhibit relativity of both kinds. What is a postulate in one may well be a theorem in the other, and a concept whose meaning is assumed in one may be introduced in the other through definition. Thus it is mere superstition, or "word magic," to suppose that any concept has the peculiar privilege of belonging at the beginning, rather than at the middle or end, of a systematic discipline. In physics, "mass" has no priority over "work" or "power"; in trigonometry, "sine" is not better qualified to be understood than "tangent"; and in biology "cell" has no unique logical prestige. For in each case definitions in other orders are possible.

When in the systematic elucidation of a field of knowledge a hitherto unfamiliar concept is explicitly introduced by definition, the definition in question is not a proposition; it is only a resolution to use the new concept as an abbreviation for some complex of older ones. Thus the utterance "Let 'p & q' be the symbol for '-($-p$ v $-q$)' " is neither true nor false. Such a resolution is called a *"nominal* definition," and is contrasted with the *"real* definition" of a concept which occurs within the system in question as a demonstrable theorem. A real definition is the analysis of a concept already understood. Thus instead of *stipulating* that "p & q" be the *symbol* for "-($-p$ v $-q$)," we might demonstrate that "p & q" *means* "-($-p$ v $-q$)"; this would assume that the concept of conjunction already occurred in the system in question, as well as the concepts of alternation and of denial. In Section 1 it was indicated that a purpose of this book was to define logic. Since it was also suggested that the idea of logic was already familiar to the reader, the intent was to promise a *real* definition of logic. On the other hand, the definition of "logical proposition" offered in Section 3 (page 11) was nominal; it was primarily a stipulation as to usage.

Now according to the principle of Conceptual Relativity, what functions in one system as a real definition may appear in another as a nominal definition. Thus there can be no unique way of settling many of the disputes in which people often engage. It is sometimes said, for example, that any *proof* of "two plus two equals four" would be gratuitous; for the *meaning* of "four" is "two plus two." Now this might indeed be the case, since it is clearly possible to define "four" nominally in this fashion. But it is also possible to give a *real* definition of "four" as "two plus two"; the only requirement is that "two" and "four" must already have been nominally defined in other terms. So whether "two plus two equals four" can be proven or not depends only on the system in which it is supposed to occur.

A real definition, then, is an analysis of a concept, while a nominal definition represents only an arbitrary stipulation. Yet from a reflective point of view it is impossible to maintain that these two functions wholly exclude each other. No nominal definition can, in fact, be entirely arbitrary. We may decide to give the name "four" to the sum of two and two; but we cannot conscionably call this sum "five." On the other hand, any real definition must in part be arbitrary, since it depends upon previous nominal definitions. The truth is that the distinction in question, like the distinction between logical and factual truth, is a philosophical idea, subject to no precise formulation. As in the case of logic itself, one must already possess the idea to understand its ramifications.

Some of the points made not only in this section but in the book as a whole can be clarified if we try to examine more closely the nature of definition in general, ignoring, for the moment, the distinction between real and nominal definitions. In the first place, the term to be defined is called the *definiendum,* and the term which does the defining is called the *definiens.* (But the difficulty of trying to discuss definition without appealing to the reader's antecedent idea of it is indicated by the fact that these words already occur on page 77!) Usually, the definiendum and definiens are joined by some form of the copulative verb, such as "is" or "are." When this is possible, the result is called an *explicit* definition. Examples are

(20.3) A triangle is a three-sided plane figure

and

(20.4) Logical truths are propositions true independently of any fact.

Sometimes, however, it is impossible or undesirable to isolate the definiens and the definiendum in such a way as to exhibit them as the subject and the predicate of a proposition.   An instance of this sort arises in the attempt to define propositional connectives like "v." In this book, there appears no statement of the form

(20.5) v is . . . .

Instead, we have been content to say

(20.6) p v q means the same as $-(-p$ & $-q)$

and to define "$\rightarrow$," "$\leftarrow\rightarrow$," and so on, in a similar fashion.   By "a similar fashion" is meant the procedure of defining the word not in isolation but rather in suitable context in which it occurs. Instead of explicitly identifying the word with a definiens, we state that its context as a whole is *equivalent* to a certain other context in which the defining words are embedded.   Definition 20.6 is thus known as a *contextual* definition.   Another contextual definition would be the result of defining "cousin" in the following manner:

(20.7) "A is a cousin of B" means the same as
        "A is the child of a brother or sister of one of B's parents."

An explicit definition of "cousin" is, indeed, also possible (see the end of Section 16, page 167), but it is more abstract and harder to understand than 20.7.

Both explicit and contextual definitions may be either real or nominal, for the distinction between real and nominal definitions has nothing to do with the *forms* of the statements in question.   It refers only to the *function* of a definition within an organized system.   The distinction we have just been discussing, however, does depend on form; an explicit definition is a proposition which may be analyzed into subject and predicate, but a contextual proposition cannot be treated in this way.

Since the majority of definitions framed for everyday purposes, as well as almost all of those in the dictionary, are explicit rather than contextual, it is useful to explore these somewhat further. Let us ask how the definiens accomplishes its purpose of specifying the meaning of the definiendum. This question has no unique answer, since there may be several ways of making a meaning clear. But an answer given by Aristotle seems to shed light on the sort of explicit definition which is most familiar to us. Aristotle distinguished four ideas which have various relationships to a given definiendum. These are *genus, differentia, property,* and *accident,* respectively. The *genus* is a class which includes the definiendum as well as other items similar to it. For example, the genus of *triangle* is *plane figure,* which of course includes quadrilaterals, pentagons, circles, and so on, as well as triangles. The *differentia* is the peculiarity of the definiendum which distinguishes it from other members of the same genus. The differentia of triangle is that it is *three-sided.* A *property* is a characteristic which belongs to the definiendum and only to it, such as, in the case of a triangle, *having an angle-sum of 180 degrees.* An *accident,* finally, is a characteristic which might belong to the definiendum, but does not necessarily belong. It is an accident of *triangle* to be equilateral.

The genus of *logical truths* is *propositions.* Its differentia is *true independently of any fact.* A property would be *implied by all propositions* (see page 94). An accident would be *involving alternation.*

Aristotle asserted that in a correct definition the definiens specifies the meaning of the definiendum by stating its genus and differentia. The combination of genus and differentia constitutes the *essence* of a term; for example, the essence of *triangle is being a plane figure and having three sides.* Aristotle thought that each term had just one essence, which means that it would fall into just one genus and would possess just one significant feature by which it could be distinguished from other members of its genus. But this view is not universally accepted today; for it is plausible to suppose that a given definiendum might fall into several equally appropriate larger classes, and bear several different marks to distinguish it from other terms. Triangles are not only plane figures; they are also figures formed by joining a certain number of points in space by straight lines. If this were taken as the genus, the differentia would have to specify that just three points are involved. To take a simpler case, a *square* is not only an equilateral rectangle, but also an equiangular rhombus. Whether a given term has one essence or many, however, Aristotle was right in supposing that it is proper to attempt to frame definitions in terms of essence.

Conversely, Aristotle thought that it would be inadequate to define a term merely by referring to one of its properties or accidents. With his rejection of *accidents* there can be no quarrel; it is certainly incorrect to define "triangle" as *"equilateral* three-sided figure." But from a modern point of view there might well be occasion to frame a legitimate definition in terms of a *property* of the definiendum. If a triangle is the one and only figure whose angle-sum is 180 degrees, then surely there can be no ambiguity in specifying "triangle" in this manner. The only difficulty might lie in the fact that perhaps *figure whose angle-sum is 180 degrees* is a less familiar idea than of *triangle* itself. But it is not necessarily the purpose of every definition to define an unfamiliar idea. It is, after all, a function of *real* definitions to analyze concepts whose meanings are assumed as already familiar in a set of postulates— to relate these concepts to others in ways that may not seem at all obvious. To discover just such unsuspected *properties* is one of the main reasons for treating knowledge in a systematic fashion. Real definitions, as we have already pointed out, are among the theorems which follow from the postulates of a given system. An example is, of course, the definition we have just been discussing: "a triangle is a figure whose angle-sum is 180 degrees." We may conclude, then, that it is proper to define a definiendum in terms of one of its properties, provided that the resulting statement functions as a real definition. On the other hand, definitions in terms of *essence* function more like *nominal definitions.* If we do not know what *triangle* is, but are acquainted with its essence, we may introduce the term into the system by referring to the latter.

In addition to the requirement that the definiens must give the essence (or, in the case of a real definition, a property) of the definiendum, and thus never merely an accident, it is often said that a good definition (a) must not be circular and (b) must not be negative. The basis of (a) is obvious; if the definiendum is already a part of the definiens, the result will be a kind of *petitio.* An example is "A triangle is a plane triangular figure." There are instances, however, in which an apparently circular definition does not really have this defect. One of the statements about logic made in Section 4 (page 19) is a case in point: "Logic is the analysis of logical propositions." The definiendum here is not really included in the definiens because "logical proposition" can itself be defined quite independently of "logic," namely, as a proposition true or false independently of any fact. On the other hand, it is doubtful that "triangular" can be defined independently of "triangle."

The difficulty with a negative definition is that in order to frame a definiens which excludes everything but the definiendum, one might have to list a very large number of excluded items. This difficulty is shown by the hopelessness of trying to define a "triangle" as "not a circle, and not a quadrilateral, and not a pentagon, and . . ." Within a limited universe of discourse, however, negative definitions are permissible; a scalene triangle, for instance, is simply "a triangle which is not isosceles and not equilateral."

Let us discuss briefly some ideas associated with essence. In connection with the explanation of *distribution* in Section 15 (page 144), essence was contrasted with *extension;* the extension of a term is the class of all objects to which the term applies. Now extension may also be contrasted with *intension;* the intension of a term consists of *all the qualities which could be meaningfully ascribed to it.* In the case of very general terms such as *triangle,* there are relatively few such qualities, since, apart from being plane and three-sided and having an angle-sum of 180 degrees, triangles in general do not have many qualities in common. Thus the intension of *triangle* is small. But its *extension* is extremely large, since the term denotes *every* triangle. If, however, we increase the intension of the term, we decrease its extension. The effect of specifying *right-angled* triangle is to denote fewer triangles than are denoted by the term *triangle* alone. To add the specification *isosceles* is to cut down extension still further. Finally, *"equilateral* isosceles right-angled triangle" has no extension at all; there are no such triangles.

The relation between intension and extension is often expressed by saying that the former varies inversely with the latter. Not only can the extension of a term be decreased by increasing its intension, but also the result of adding to extension will be to diminish intension. For the more objects we collect together the fewer will be the qualities they possess in common. Some words refer to *all* objects, for example, "thing" or "entity." But things in general have nothing in common; thus the term has no intension.

There are, however, exceptions to the rule that intension varies inversely with extension. Consider the series

(20.8) Organisms, animal, vertebrate, mammal, rational, living, American, less than 300 years old.

Each term of 20.8, after the first, increases the intension and decreases the extension of its predecessor—except for the last term. This last increases the intension of "living Americans," but does not diminish its extension, since there are exactly as many living Americans under 300 years old as there are living Americans.

Usually the intension of a term involves more qualities than its essence, and 20.8 serves to illustrate this point as well. If, as many philosophers have thought, *being a rational animal* is the essence of the term *man,* then this essence makes no explicit reference to the qualities *organism, vertebrate,* and *mammal* which are also included, among many others, in the intension of *man*. This points to the fact that a definition is not the same thing as an exhaustive specification. To define, it is sufficient to mention only those qualities of the definiendum which are relevant to the purpose at hand.

EXERCISES

A. 1. Does the principle of Postulational Relativity mean that a proposition which is true in one system may be false in another? Explain your answer.

2. Explain how Postulational Relativity is exemplified by the two sets of rules for the syllogism given in Section 19.

3. Given the truth-tables for "*p* v *q*" and for -*p*, we can prove that the truth-table for "*p* & *q*" is

$$p \ \& \ q$$
$$\text{T T T}$$
$$\text{F F T}$$
$$\text{T F F}$$
$$\text{F F F}$$

But given this truth-table and the one for -*p*, we can prove that the truth-table for "*p* v *q*" is

$$p \ \text{v} \ q$$
$$\text{T T T}$$
$$\text{F T T}$$
$$\text{T T F}$$
$$\text{F F F}$$

How is Postulational Relativity exemplified by this situation?

4. When the assumption is made that "All *S* is *P*" and "No *S* is *P*" are both true, it can easily be shown that *there is no S*. And when the assumption is made that "All *S* is *P*" is true, but there is no *S*, it follows that no *S* is *P*. Does this situation exemplify Postulational Relativity?

5. If the two premises of a syllogism are regarded as postulates and the conclusion as a theorem, is it possible to exhibit Postulational Relativity? Explain.

6. Does the principle of Conceptual Relativity mean that a concept which has a certain meaning in one system may have some other meaning in another system? Explain your answer.

7. The conventional approach to the rules of the syllogism assumes the meaning of the concept of *distribution*. It defines "a universal proposition" as "one whose subject is distributed," and "a negative proposition" as "one whose predicate is distributed." Proceeding on the assumption that a particular proposition is just one that is not universal, and that an affirmative proposition is just one that is not negative, one may then infer that the subject of a particular proposition is undistributed, and that the predicate of an affirmative proposition is undistributed.

   But it is also possible to assume *undistributed* as an undefined concept, to define "particular proposition" and "affirmative proposition" in terms of that, and thence to prove that the subject of a universal proposition and the predicate of a negative proposition are distributed.

   Is this a case of Conceptual Relativity? Explain.

8. Boggs: I think Diggs should be removed from his position on the School Board. He's a Communist, you know.
   Meggs: Those are strong words, my friend. What *proof* do you have that he is a Communist?
   Boggs: I don't *have* to prove it. Diggs has said in public that he favors UNESCO; and *by definition,* anyone that favors UNESCO is a Communist.
   To what extent, if any, does the distinction between real and nominal definitions clarify the issue here?

9. It is sometimes said that any definition is either trivial or false. For if the definiens has the same meaning as the

definiendum, the definition is trivial; while if the definiens has a different meaning from the definiendum, the definition is false.

(i) What light is shed on this difficulty by the notion of Conceptual Relativity? Would it make sense, for example, to argue that whether the definiens does or does not "have the same meaning" as the definiendum depends upon the position of the definition within a given system?

(ii) Could the problem be solved by making the distinction between nominal and real definitions? Where definiens and definiendum have the same meaning, must the definition be trivial? Where they have different meanings, must the definition be incorrect?

10. Illustrate Postulational and Conceptual Relativity in terms of two simple sets of postulates of your own devising. These need not be complete, or even precisely equivalent. (It may be suggested that a simple but plausible set of postulates might take the form of a miniature national constitution, a set of rules for a game, a set of rules for deciding which of several possible courses of action to take in everyday life, or a simple statement of the fundamental laws of a science.)

B. Evaluate each of the following definitions. Where you decide that the definition is faulty, refer to one or more of the following possible defects.

(a) The genus is not correctly stated. (Is the stated genus more inclusive than it should be? Or is it too narrow?)

(b) The differentia is not correctly stated. (Is the stated differentia sufficient to distinguish the definiendum from other members of the same genus? Does it necessarily attach to all instances of the definiendum?)

(c) An accident of the definiendum, rather than its essence, is used to define it.

(d) The definition is circular.

(e) The definition is negative.

(f) The definition is defective in some other way.

1. A square is an equilateral four-sided figure.

2. A square is a rectangle the area of which is the product of its base times its altitude.

3. A square is a rectangle the base of which does not differ from its altitude.

4. A square is an equiangular rectangle.

5. A square is the shape of the Square of Opposition.

6. A bird is a flying animal.

7. A bird is an avian animal having the body feathered and the forelimbs modified to form wings.

8. A bird is an animal other than a fish, amphibian, reptile, or mammal.

9. A bird is a vertebrate other than a fish, amphibian, reptile, or mammal.

10. A bird is a warm-blooded animal having the body feathered and the forelimbs modified to form wings.

11. A table is anything with a smooth, flat top supported by uprights.

12. A table is a wooden article of furniture with a smooth, flat top supported by four legs.

13. A table is an article of furniture used to support other objects.

14. A table is an article of furniture with a smooth, flat top supported by legs.

15. A table is an article of furniture supported by legs.

16. "A robs B" means the same as "A takes from B an article which does not belong to A."

17. "A robs B" means the same as "A steals from B an article worth more than $100."

18. "A robs B" means the same as "A assaults B without the direct intent of either injuring B or compelling B to perform an action which he would not otherwise perform."

19. "A robs B" means the same as "A steals an article from B by means of force or fear."

20. "A robs B" means the same as "If arrested and convicted, A will be sentenced on a charge of robbery."

21. A Communist is any person who disagrees with the present form of government.

22. A Communist is any person who is not in favor of capitalism.
23. A Communist is any person who associates with Communists.
24. A Communist is any person who invokes the Fifth Amendment.
25. A Communist is any intellectual who was in New York or Hollywood during the depression.

C. Rearrange each of the following series so that the terms appear in the order of increasing intension.

1. Syllogism, *AAA* in the first figure, argument, proposition, complex proposition.
2. Valid argument, truth, conditional argument, logical truth, propositional argument, indirect proof.
3. Invalid argument, fallacy, illicit process of the minor, logical error.
4. Novel, means of communication, by Dumas, book, *The Three Musketeers,* printed matter.
5. Vegetable, Rome Beauty, organism, object, fruit, apple.

SUPPLEMENTARY READINGS

1. Irving M. Copi, *Introduction to Logic,* New York, The Macmillan Company, 1953, Ch. 4.

2. Lionel Ruby, *Logic: An Introduction,* New York, J. B. Lippincott Company, 1950, Pt. 1, Ch. 5.

3. Monroe C. Beardsley, *Practical Logic,* New York, Prentice-Hall, Inc., 1950, Ch. 6.

4. Max Black, *Critical Thinking,* New York, Prentice-Hall, Inc., 2d ed., 1952, Ch. 11.

5. Ralph M. Eaton, *General Logic,* New York, Charles Scribner's Sons, 1931, Pt. II, Chs. VI-VII.

On Non-Euclidean Geometry

6. Nicholas Lobachevski, *The Theory of Parallels* (Tr. George Bruce Halsted), Chicago, Open Court Publishing Co., 1914.

7. Lillian R. Lieber, *Non-Euclidean Geometry, or Three Moons in Mathesis,* Lancaster, Pa., The Science Press Printing Co., 2d ed., 1940.

On the Logical Foundations of Arithmetic

8. Bertrand Russell, *Introduction to Mathematical Philosophy,* London, George Allen & Unwin, Ltd., 2d ed., 1920, Chs. I-III.

21

The Grounds of Belief

Emphasis was given in Section 5 (page 26), and again in Section 19 (page 199), to the maxim "Not every proposition can be proved." This maxim, if taken seriously, should produce a salutary kind of skepticism, for it invites distrust of the attempt to reduce all knowledge to deductive logic. In order to prove anything at all, one must at some point assert at least one proposition without proof. The attempt to draw *this* proposition into the deductive system, by proving *it* too, inevitably leads to a dilemma. Suppose p is the unproved proposition in question. Either the proof of p requires some further unproved proposition, say q, or it does not. If it does, we have not improved our position. If it does not, then this means that p can be satisfactorily demonstrated in terms of propositions already proved, say s and r. But to the extent that they are already proved, their proofs must assume p. Thus p cannot be inferred from s and r; an attempt to infer it would constitute a *petitio*.

It is important, however, to be sure that one understands exactly what the maxim "You can't prove everything" means. It does not call for an unqualified skepticism, since it does not imply that there are certain fixed propositions which will never be proved. Rather, it only asserts that the formulation of any deductive system depends upon some or other propositions which are not theorems *in that system*. In other words, you can't prove everything *all at once,* within the scope of a single system. But this is not to say "You can't prove everything *one at a time.*" And, in fact, as the discussion of Postulational Relativity in Section 20 strongly suggests, *any* proposition *can* be proved, given the appropriate assumptions and provided the proposition is true. If the proposition is false, of course, we would not be able to assert every member of a set of premises implying it, as proving it would require. No valid proof could have all true premises but a false conclusion.

But the question arises, "How shall we identify a premise, assumption or postulate as true?" One obvious method for ascertaining that a proposition is true is to prove the proposition. That method applies, however, only to theorems. And, as we have just shown, while the postulates of any given system may be capable of being proved within some *other* system, they cannot be proved within the very system in which they operate as postulates. This shows that any organized system of knowledge involves more than one method of identifying truth. There is, on the one hand, the process of showing that a proposition is true by proving it, or of showing that it is false by disproving it. Let us call this the *Method of Proof.* On the other hand there are the procedures— what they are, and whether one or many, has not yet been touched on in this book—for deciding whether an assumption or postulate is true or false. Let us see to what extent we can describe this second method or sort of method.

The possibility of a further method for identifying a proposition as true or false is suggested by the fact that in Part One we somehow distinguished logically true from logically false propositions without resorting to proof. But even if we could clearly describe the method used there, it would not be helpful to us now. Since logical truths imply only other logical truths, and since the theorems which occur in systematic treatments of science and other areas of knowledge are not logical truths, it follows that the postulates for such areas of knowledge are not logically true. Besides, we never described the procedure involved in distinguishing logical truth from logical falsehood. All that we did accomplish in this connection was to show how *logical* propositions may be distinguished from *factual* ones, namely, through the occurrence of variables. But within the domain of logical propositions, we relied only on the reader's intuition or common sense. It was common sense, for example, that led us to decide that "All black cats are black" is true but "Some black cats are not black" is false.

We seek, then, a way of recognizing *factual* truth and falsity; for postulates, not being logical, must be factual propositions. Thus for the first time during the course of this book we are explicitly concerned with factual propositions, and therefore encroaching upon the subject-matter of inductive logic. This incursion is justified only by the desire to round off the study of postulates with which we have been concerned in the present part.

If we are able, on the basis of intuition alone, to decide whether a *logical* proposition is true or false, why may we not use the same sort of intuition in accepting or rejecting our postulates? Following the great nineteenth-century American logician and philosopher Charles Sanders Peirce, let us call the procedure of verification which rests on intuition the *Method of Tenacity*. This consists in clinging tenaciously to a belief and not permitting it to be subjected to any critical examination. For if we genuinely suppose that it is the intuitive attractiveness of the belief that guarantees its truth, then we shall be unwilling to defer to any other standard of truth. The words "prejudice" and "faith" both refer to the Method of Tenacity, one in a disapproving sense and the other approvingly. It is a part of the very meaning of both words that neither sort of belief is, from the point of view of the believer, open to question.

As Peirce points out, this method is not without its advantages. "Men who pursue it are distinguished for their decision of character." * Indeed, it is difficult to see how the Method of Tenacity could be completely avoided in the realm of practical action. But

* "The Fixation of Belief," in *Popular Science Monthly,* 1877. All quotations used in this section are from the same article.

in matters of scientific thought, rather than unreflective activity, it is defective. "The man who adopts it will find that other men think differently from him, and it will be apt to occur to him, in some saner moment, that their opinions are quite as good as his own, and this will shake his confidence in his belief." To organize knowledge systematically is not merely a purpose of the individual but also one of society at large. "Unless we make ourselves hermits, we shall necessarily influence each other's opinions."

Since society is concerned with organized knowledge, then why not let society itself be the arbiter of truth? The procedure of identifying a proposition as true or false by referring to standards imposed by society Peirce calls the *Method of Authority*. A postulate accepted on the basis of this method is often called a *dogma*. Dogmas are the elements of "orthodox" belief. Such belief need not, of course, emanate from society as a whole; it may as readily reflect the assertions of men or books regarded as authoritative.

The Method of Authority is essential to social cohesion. Any social group presupposes at least a common set of interests, whose validity is unquestioned by that group. The belief that these interests are valid thus constitutes an orthodoxy. But if it is assumed that *all* propositions fall within the scope of this Method, serious dangers are likely to arise; three of these dangers are emphasized by Peirce. One of them occurs as a result of the problem of dealing with those who disagree with the accepted standards. The danger is in the obvious way of solving this problem: "Let the people turn out and tar-and-feather such men, or let inquisitions be made into the manner of thinking of suspected persons, and when they are found guilty of forbidden beliefs, let them be subject to some signal punishment." Ostracism and exile are other solutions. But the Method of Authority can, in itself, offer no *rational* means of settling disputes.

Another difficulty is that "no institution *can* undertake to regulate opinions upon every subject. Only the most important ones can be attended to, and on the rest men's minds must be left to the action of natural causes." Such causes include other methods for identifying truth. And when society attempts to remedy the situation by declaring a new official dogma regarding a hitherto undecided question, this declaration cannot, in the nature of the case, rest upon authority. Other methods are thus necessarily presupposed by the Method of Authority itself.

Finally, there will inevitably be members of society who know that "men in other countries and in other ages have held to very different doctrines from those which they themselves have been brought up to believe; and (who) cannot help seeing that it is the mere accident of their having been taught as they have, and of their having been surrounded with the manners and associations they have, that has caused them to believe as they do and not far differently." Viewed on this basis, other systems of authority seem every bit as reasonable as one's own.

Reasonableness thus becomes a criterion for identifying an assumption as true or false. And a belief is, in this sense, "reasonable" if it is capable of overcoming the limitations of the Method of Authority; which is to say that it must be common to all men and capable of shedding light on all subjects. Through the course of history many beliefs have been seized upon as reasonable in these terms. They have generally served as the postulates of philosophical systems. Examples are: "Every event has a cause," "All men are created equal," "Virtue is its own reward." Not all such beliefs are, of course, universally accepted. But it is argued that if all men *were* fully rational, these are the beliefs that they *would* accept. It is difficult to conceal the *petitio* in this argument.

Peirce calls this method for identifying true assumptions the *A Priori Method*. The method is *a priori* in the sense that it makes no fundamental appeal to experience. The postulate "Every event has a cause," for example, is generally intended as more than a generalization from past experience; it is rather supposed to operate as a way of making sense of experience itself.

The advantage of the *A Priori* Method is in the apparent ease and assurance with which it reaches its conclusions. If the mark of a true proposition is only that it be "agreeable to reason," we have but to consult our own sense of what is rational to determine whether a given proposition is true.   But the defect of this method, according to Peirce, is that the concept of rationality has itself no genuine universality; it has varied from age to age and from culture to culture.   The modern quantum physicist, for example, must have a different notion of what is agreeable to reason than his predecessors did, since he rejects the thesis that every event must have a cause.   The ancient Greeks regarded as a clear and indisputable deliverance of reason the conclusion that not all men are created equal.   And it is a part of the twentieth-century conception of rationality to see nothing essentially irrational in the possibility that virtue might never be rewarded in any way.   Like taste, the concept of reason has undergone development.

But development, while it is a process which eliminates the effect of some casual circumstances, only magnifies that of others.   This Method, therefore, does not differ in a very essential way from that of authority.   The government may not have lifted its finger to influence my convictions; I may have been left outwardly quite free to choose, we will say, between monogamy and polygamy, and, appealing to [reason] only, I may have concluded that the latter practice is in itself licentious.   But when I come to see that the chief obstacle to the spread of Christianity among a people of as high culture as the Hindus has been a conviction of the immorality of our way of treating women, I cannot help seeing that, though governments do not interfere, sentiments in their development will be very greatly determined by accidental causes.

The only ultimately satisfactory method for selecting the true postulates of organized knowledge must, then, be one which overcomes this defect.   It must be a procedure "by which our beliefs may be determined by nothing human, but by some external permanency—by something upon which our thinking has no effect." And this permanency "must be something which affects, or might affect, every man."   Peirce feels that the method which could meet these requirements is that used in science.   He therefore

identifies it as the *Method of Scientific Investigation*.   Its true universality is exhibited in the fact that "everybody uses (it) about a
great many things, and only ceases to use it when he does not know
how to apply it."   And "experience of the method has not led us
to doubt it, but, on the contrary, scientific investigation has had
the most wonderful triumphs in the way of settling opinion."

The Method of Scientific Investigation is the only one capable
of testing its own results.   To presume to test intuition is, as we
have pointed out, already to presuppose some method over and
above that of tenacity; an intuition is just an intuition, and cannot,
in its own terms, be right or wrong.   Similarly with the Method of
Authority: "the only test *on that method* is what the state thinks;
so that it cannot pursue the method wrongly."   The same defect is
associated with the *A Priori* Method.   For if reason is the ultimate
court of appeal, we cannot question its deliverances except by appealing to some source of knowledge lying beyond it.   But for the
Method of Scientific Investigation, "the test of whether I am truly
following the method is not an immediate appeal to my feelings and
purposes, but, on the contrary, itself involves the application of the
method.   Hence it is that bad reasoning as well as good reasoning
is possible; and this fact is the foundation of the practical side of
logic."   By "the practical side of logic," Peirce meant what we
might call "the *factual* side," that is, *inductive* logic.

One cannot accurately *define* the Method of Scientific Investigation except in terms of an extended discussion of the standards of
scientific truth, just as one cannot define logic except by discussing
at length the standards of logical truth.   Such a real definition of
scientific investigation falls beyond the scope of this book.   But
that is not necessarily an obstacle to our present attempt to *com-
pare* the Method of Scientific Investigation with other methods.
For if, at the beginning of this work, it was safe to presume that
the reader was already familiar with the meaning of "logic," in the
sense that a nominal definition of logic in terms of ideas *more*
familiar to him would have been impossible to offer, then it is
also safe to presume that he is already familiar with the meaning

of "science."   Indeed, if a person totally lacked any conception of
scientific procedure it would be fully as impossible to implant that
conception in his mind merely by enumerating the criteria of scientific truth as it would be to make an illogical person logical merely
by confronting him with truth-tables, Venn Diagrams, and so on.
Science is not just a collection of methods, any more than logic is.
Both science and logic are modes of experience whose full significance can be grasped only by one who has actually participated in
the experience.

Science is not only a *mode* of experience; it also involves a type
of *reference* to experience which is absent from all other methods.
In particular, the Method of Scientific Investigation essentially involves a reference to that kind of experience which is gained
through observation and experimentation.   And it is clear that no
experience of this kind would be relevant to the pronouncements
of intuition, authority, or reason, as such.   The relationship between scientific observation and scientific theory is so complex that
it would be foolish to attempt to pontificate upon it in these last
paragraphs.   However it is clear that the postulates of organized
scientific knowledge must either be directly capable of experimental
confirmation or disconfirmation, or else must imply theorems dependent in the same way upon experimentation.

We may conclude, then, that the Method of Scientific Investigation is the only ultimately satisfactory way of identifying the postulates upon which organized knowledge rests.   But this is not to
reject the other methods, which are essential to the selection of
postulates for activities other than knowledge.   Thus the Method
of Tenacity furnishes the unquestioned assumptions of practical
conduct.   The Method of Authority provides the foundations of
loyalty to a social group.   And the *A Priori* Method yields the
basic postulates of philosophical vision.

SUPPLEMENTARY READINGS

1. Max Black, *Critical Thinking,* New York, Prentice-Hall, Inc., 2d
ed., 1952, Ch. 13.

2. Morris R. Cohen and Ernest Nagel, *An Introduction to Logic and Scientific Method,* New York, Harcourt, Brace and Company, Inc., 1934, Chs. X, XI.

3. Ralph M. Eaton, *General Logic,* New York, Charles Scribner's Sons, 1931, Pt. IV, Ch. IV.

General

4. Aristotle, *Posterior Analytics,* Bk. I, Chs. I, II, XVIII, XXXI; Bk. II, Ch. XIX.

5. Immanuel Kant, *Critique of Pure Reason,* "Preface" to 2d ed.

6. John Stuart Mill, *A System of Logic,* Bk. III.

7. John Dewey, *Logic: The Theory of Inquiry,* New York, Henry Holt and Company, 1938, Pt. I.

8. Norman Campbell, *What Is Science?* New York, Dover Publications, Inc., 1952.

9. James B. Conant, *On Understanding Science,* New Haven, Yale University Press, 1947.

Index

Index

This book may be kept

FOURTEEN DAYS
A fine of TWO CENTS will be charged for each day
the Book is kept over time.

OC 9 67			